Karen

Suc...
Step
Parenting

—

BERNARDINE COVERLEY

BLOOMSBURY

First published 1996 by Bloomsbury Publishing Plc,
2 Soho Square,
London W1V 6HB

Copyright © 1996 Bernardine Coverley

The moral right of the author has been asserted

A copy of the CIP entry for this book is available from
the British Library

ISBN 0 7475 2178 6

10 9 8 7 6 5 4 3 2 1

Designed by Hugh Adams, AB3
Typeset by Hewer Text Composition Services,
Edinburgh
Printed in Great Britain by Cox & Wyman Ltd,
Reading, Berkshire

Introduction

I ENJOYED stepfamily life, it was the most hard working and satisfying period of my life and that encouraged me to write this book. I didn't plan to, it sort of sprang upon me when I heard an editor say she was looking for new titles and I suggested what came into my mind in a spontaneous and rather light-hearted way. As a freelance journalist, I suggest ideas all the time and many fall by the wayside, not this one.

My stepfamily was made up of my two daughters aged ten and eight and me together with Christopher and his three daughters, aged ten, seven and four years old and, later, our son. I enjoyed the company of my three stepdaughters. I loved seeing the children dressing up, making things, having pets, getting something out of life in a big family as well as watching each individual grow up. There were plenty of dilemmas when I wished I knew what to do but more often than not I thought we were wonderful. That is not to say we did not have unresolved situations.

It was also an exhausting time. I couldn't resist doing everything and I was horrified when a neighbour suggested I make a small retreat, a corner which was just mine, somewhere in the house. I had thrown myself into the role of stepmother so thoroughly that I had lost my sense of being a separate adult.

So many families nowadays are stepfamilies and they deserve recognition and support. We exist and do a good job. I wanted to write this book because I still value those years. I know many stepfamilies feel that they are not valued by anyone else, rather that they are ignored. And within those families the bonds do not cease when the children are grown-up, the relationships continue.

The links between all of us in our family continue to evolve.

However, when the contract for the book arrived, I felt stunned at the thought of looking at my past again to see what worked and what didn't. I began to doubt what had seemed fine at the time. We move on and the past looks a little different at each backward review. The present is more important. But it will always be true that I did love being a stepmother.

I wrote this book from past experience and present reflection, for everyone who wants to think about adults and children getting used to living together and then getting the best from it. I talked with families who lived in rural areas and cities, rented homes and owned homes. I talked to people with money, people who hadn't got much, families where religion was important and families with mixed cultural or ethnic roots, second generation Irish and Caribbean.

It isn't aimed only at the step parent but equally at the parent because I believe, as well as from talking with other parents in stepfamilies, it can also be the parent that tries to be all things to all people and who consequently suffers a sense of divided loyalty.

After being a tight unit of three with me at the apex I had other objects of affection and at times I felt, 'Can I follow my instincts or do I have to be scrupulously fair and balanced?' From other mothers I have heard the same dilemma, who commands the first loyalty, the children or the new husband?

So it isn't only the step parent who needs reassurance on a new way of living. And many parents watch their child go to visit another stepfamily to stay with the other birth parent. A stepfamily is everyone and extends beyond the two adults and the children. Adapting within this new family isn't one person's 'problem' or specific to the adult entering the family home or unit and it shouldn't be.

Also it can be illuminating to hear another point of view so there are chapters from the stepchildren and from the other parent. However distant they may be from the stepfamily, the other parents always have some effect and the less we close ranks to leave the birth parent to their new life, the less pressure is put on the child. In fact I rang my step daughter's mother to confirm my memory that we co-operated very fruitfully was correct. 'Yes,' she said laughing, 'in spite of hearing that with you everything was perfect.'

My husband and I started off well as a couple, sharing housework and cooking and having time to go out together and have conversations about subjects totally unrelated to our family. The children loved hearing about our evenings dancing in Brighton or the latest gossip after a meal with friends. But as time went on it was all too easy to forget to reserve space and time for us without children and without the other people who come in and out attracted by the activity of a large family.

Even so, I remember those years as ones where I became good at some things having learnt by being rushed into things because they had to be done or they had to be done more thoroughly. I learnt to make huge meals, grow vegetables, help fix things and drive a van.

If I wanted to continue my own interests, – I was completing a teacher training course, I'm passionate about reading and I had long-standing friends, – they couldn't be haphazard or only spontaneous because they would be submerged by all the other demands. I had homework to complete on time, preparation to do, I needed my best friend, who lived in Scotland, to come and stay.

Could I still spend my money in the way I wanted and take my children out to things we were used to doing? Not always, and I gave up some customs and treats that would have done me and my children good to hold on to. It was confusing at times.

Some aspects of my life I threw over happily. I stopped struggling to survive as a single parent against the world. I remember being thrilled to be at home with the baby and doing housework! Before, I had to think about children, work and money. Now I had someone to share responsibilities with. I didn't have to do it all on my own.

As I began to talk to people, even before starting to gather material for the book, I was surprised at how frequently the words 'difficulties' and 'problems' were mentioned. I began to think I had imagined my own mainly good, not necessarily easy, but definitely good experience. Was it all a rosy illusion?

Someone else in the same situation with the same people might have hated it.

There were certainly things I could have done differently; give my children more time, for example, nothing major, just special attention. And there are other more knotty reflections I could spend time on, wishing I had been stronger, calmer and so on. We all know how endless that can be.

Our neighbours had very different reactions to living near a stepfamily with six children plus pets, plus van under frequent repair. For some we were the problem. Our nearest neighbours, Margaret and Darby, were real fans, others, luckily further off, regarded us as akin to white trash. Obviously not all stepfamilies are large. Some are parent, child and step parent and from the outside no one would notice. But we were highly visible and worse, probably highly audible.

Just as problems were mentioned by the adults I interviewed, stepchildren brought up how they felt about themselves as the moveable object of attention but not consultation. The children, some of them grown up now, also spoke of becoming good friends with acquired brothers or sisters, and new babies are loved more often than not.

This is not to deny hatred and jealousy and quarrels because these are part of the package and can be fierce and damaging. All our children had their own views, and rivalries too, some of which I didn't want to face. But compare the myth of the perfect nuclear family and the secret and not so secret flaws in that. Divorce and separation are common and in the open. Before the mid 20th century the family was just as complex but hypocrisy ruled along with fear of what the neighbours said and the religion decreed.

At a conference, I listened to a researcher speaking of elderly people, who would have been born before and during the First World War. His questions revealed how few of these people had lived with both parents in a conventional family.

Hearing about the histories of people from my grandparents' generation brought to mind the rarely spoken of facts in my own background. I know, almost by chance, in passing, that my grandmother must have been married twice and that some of her children would have had a stepfather and half siblings.

In some part of my mind I knew something of this, whispered things I overheard as a child about banished uncles, half answers to my questions from my grandmother. And yet this man must have had a lasting influence in the family. I also knew without even being able to put it into thoughts that this was a forbidden subject.

On my mother's 80th birthday I joked about my father being spoilt as he was the only boy and, as she was a little tipsy, she contradicted me saying that he had three half brothers. By this time I was myself in a second relationship and began to understand the enormously critical weight I felt from my father and the effect my life must have had on him. I believe he saw me acting out a parallel life to his mother especially as he had tried so hard to move into a more secure and conventional world. And what was this all about? It was the fact that my grandmother was hopeful enough to have another man, have more children and had loved again.

STEPFAMILY, the National Stepfamily Association say that many of their calls are from those who do not consider themselves part of a stepfamily even though they have chosen this organization to ring. The image of the one family model made up of father, mother plus two children is so firmly etched on our minds that we cannot see what else is out there.

I mention my grandmother because all family relationships exist below the surface and cannot be governed by good intentions only or by doing the right thing. Families, like any cluster of people, have a group life too and the more open we are as adults and the more we accept each child and adult as they are, the healthier the life of the family. It is when we do not acknowledge or understand the hidden past, one family member may act out suppressed fears triggering anger and divided loyalties. When this happens, as it inevitably does at some stage in every sort of family, I am a great believer, if less than a great practitioner, in assertion as a way of coping. Personally, I feel much more at home with self-help networks and am a touch resistant to anything institutional with experts and a lot of theories.

However, I also believe most of us need to feel supported when we are part of a stepfamily and getting that support is not a sign of being 'not good enough'. What gives me strength and confidence will not be the natural way for you but no-one has to struggle proudly in isolation living a new version of the perfect family.

It is hard going at times because we *are* trying to be good and caring parents, and we know the children did not choose. It is our choice and that makes us vulnerable. Have we done the right thing after all? We did not doubt and question so much when our first family was growing up. Now we seek to actively understand how this can work for the other members of this new family as well as for ourselves.

I am not an expert. I wrote this book because I had experience and because I believe if you're doing something for love, however difficult, it's got to be enjoyable, got to be more than hard work and high-mindedness. For the rest, I talked and listened to dozens of people, stepmothers, stepfathers, step-children, step-grandparents and I looked back at many families I had known and realized that stepfamilies were everywhere. I also feel strongly that we all need refreshing even by the briefest moment away from our beloved.

I am a grandmother now and I look forward to being a stepgrandmother. Twenty five years after I met my daughter's schoolfriend and then her father and sisters, the one definite statement I can make with confidence is that all the children 'turned out well'.

So read on and take what is useful. This book is merely a map of the landscape with all its possible avenues and its rocky bits and the occasional clear view. You will all take your own route.

Bernardine Coverley
January 1996

Contents

Chapter 1
Facts Myths Stereotypes

---

stepfamily (n) a family created by two adult partners one or each of whom already has a child from a previous relationship; the offspring from a former marriage ended by separation, death or divorce, a former co-habitation, or an extra-marital affair. A stepfamily may include a resident stepchild(ren) or a partially resident stepchild(ren) who live primarily with their other birth parent, and a child(ren) of the two adults who is a half-sibling to the stepchild(ren). The stepfamily relationship exists even when the adults and children have not met each other or lived together and extends to grandparents, aunts, uncles and cousins. (From STEPFAMILY, the National Step-family Association.

There are over a million children growing up in full-time stepfamilies. Many other children live in part-time stepfamilies or visit a parent who is living with or is remarried to someone who does not have any responsibility for them, who is not a step-parent but who is, 'Dad's girl friend' or 'Mum's bloke'. 8% of all dependent children live in a stepfamily. If that doesn't sound many, turn it into numbers and it then becomes approximately 2½ million children who are part of a full-time or a part-time stepfamily. In 1994, the beleaguered Child Support Agency complained that their brief had been made all the more compli-cated by discovering that more stepfamilies existed than was expected.

FACTS

- 1 in 3 marriages is a remarriage
- 1 in 7 marriages are of 2 divorced partners
- 299,000 marriages in 1993, the lowest level for 50 years
- no way to record the total number of stepfamilies
- There are 7 times more full-time stepfathers than stepmothers
- 52% of full-time stepfamilies have a new baby
- 1 in 12 dependent children live in stepfamilies
- 1 in 3 children are born to unmarried parents

Statistics can only give certain indications of what the nation is doing and, now that many first marriages are faltering, there are no official statistics for the number of stepfamilies in our society. The 299,000 weddings in 1993 was the lowest number recorded for 50 years and, of these, a third were remarriages for one or both partners. The word remarriage is used frequently to mean second and third marriages.

Human beings appear to be infinitely optimistic; when relationships break up we are so willing to try again, and that must be good. But romance, hope and serial monogamy lead to some very complicated and demanding relationships both emotionally and economically. At least we can remind ourselves when the going gets tough that there are many like us.

Stepfamilies are now so common that popular images and the real facts have not kept up with each other. A step-parent used to act as a parent, in the place of a dead or absent parent. That is not automatically the case now. Children are more likely to remain in touch with the birth parent and are less likely to need a replacement. There isn't an empty space to fill, left by divorce, death or abandonment. However, the birth parent may not always be around after a divorce or separation and there are many variations of the family group created by a new relationship or a remarriage. What happens in one stepfamily is not the same as in another. What works for one stepfamily is not right for all stepfamilies.

Becoming a 'step-parent' states a commitment to a partner's children and a willingness to care for, love, bring up, and guide them through the obstacles and pangs of growing up, while also taking a place in a family unit that already exists. When another person becomes part of an established group, even a group of two, that group changes in ways that can not be foreseen.

The children do not always have the same point of view as the adults. A teenager refused the 'step' label insisting that she didn't need another 'parent' of any sort. The adults in her family identified with the useful word, step-parent because they needed to describe their role in the family to the outside world.

I still use the 'step' word to describe myself and I use 'stepdaughter' to introduce any of the three young women that I used to bring up. I didn't really think about it or notice when I began to use it, I know I didn't want to let go of it when they weren't children any longer. Now I'm not sure how I would describe us as a family or as related people if they were children. It's a practical label because I want people to know we continue to have an important connection, that we are not 'just good friends'.

STEPFAMILY MYTHS

- That there is a traditional/nuclear/normal family
- Remarriage means being a traditional family again
- Second-best families
- The wicked stepmother – myth or part truth
- Given time, all members of a stepfamily will love each other
- When a stepfamily is created after the death of a partner, it will be easier than after a divorce
- Divorce, inevitably, harms all children forever
- Visiting stepchildren are easier to cope with than live-in ones
- Partners can love each other so much that the problems will be easily dealt with

3

Old Myth
Better to have no contact with a parent who has left

New Myth
Contact at all costs with a parent who has left
© National Stepfamily Association

The hierarchy of dad, mum and children has blurred to a sometimes bewildering array of current and ex-spouses, half- and step-siblings as people marry and remarry. I use the word marriage as a convenience since what used to be called common law marriage is, well, common, even though it does not have the legal rights of marriage.

It is normal to be a stepfamily and not want to be compared interminably to a 'nuclear family'. If that was so good then most stepfamilies would not have come into being but, before we get too keen on the idea that it is nuclear families who constantly explode and scatter debris, statistics show that plenty of second families also split up. If the notorious figure of one in three for marital breakdown is topped by the two in three of second marriages, then what happens to these new family relationships after separation? Unlike birth parents and children whose natural relationship is taken for granted, that of the step-parents and children may not be so. And yet, why should that bond be broken too? This does not deny that being a step-parent is stressful for some and it can be a tremendous relief to lay down the responsibility but this may lead to a more relaxed and spontaneous contact with the stepchild. It is reassuring for adults as well as children to know small simple gestures of remembering or appreciation are worthwhile. If you are no longer a step-parent officially, through divorce or separation, that doesn't wipe out the past or the bond that remains.

The Goodies And Baddies

Step-parenting carries with it a huge moral burden. So many step-parents, especially women, respond as if they have to be perfect and somehow make everything right. As if there is a right, a proper pattern. Perhaps we long to create a sense of harmony out of different tastes and family customs and that too can often turn into having rigid ideas or a desperate attempt to control. Rather than accepting that life worth living is also tough at times, we look for the baddies to blame and that includes ourselves. Aren't stepfamilies' problems self-inflicted? After all no-one asked us to get involved with a parent. The other baddies are, naturally enough, the predecessors. The tempting idea that any problems or difference is the result of 'their mother's' or 'their father's' wild, wicked and selfish ways lies behind much of the step-parent seeking to impose an ideal. 'Pamela says I'm a prig. You don't think that, do you?' He asked aggrievedly after one of those phone calls and, although I looked at his hurt expression with affection and replied with the appropriate balm, 'of course not', I knew exactly what my predecessor meant. It is easy to be holier-than-thou towards the non-custodial parent.

Church State And Family

The first official stepfamily in Britain, through divorce, was created by a notorious monarch, Henry the Eighth. His wife-changing habits could only be legally endorsed by God through his representative here on earth, the Pope. Divorce was not permitted by the Catholic Church. An annulment, a pronouncement that a marriage had not truly existed, was all that was permitted. It was achieved with great difficulty and annulments could not be granted one after the other. Political alliances also came into the scene. Eventually, Henry, tired of the intrigue required to replace one wife with another, founded the Church of England which, as its head, he could control. Rather ironic then that the modern Church of England expresses dismay at what is seen as the rapidly crumbling family structure, and this in spite of divorce and remarriage by Church of England vicars.

> *Mark, as stepfather, brought an added element to his pastoral work as a vicar but, equally, he was vulnerable to criticism from traditional moralists. Fortunately, he found that within the church body there are many approaches to the problematic area of human relations.*

'I wondered what the reaction would be in the parish when I married a woman with four children. I knew no-one could fail to like Jill but I also know that some parishioners are very traditional and might not accept a stepfamily where one party has been divorced. In the end only two parishioners left to worship elsewhere.'

However, Mark accepts there will be limits to his professional promotion at least in the near future,: 'Bishops decide the future of their employees so we were told that some parishes wouldn't want us. Attitudes are changing though, modern life is like this.'

The image of a stepfather vicar does not fit in with the image the church wants to present, but a vicar like Mark is, in practice, a valuable role model for local churchgoers now, and may do the Church's image a favour later. For many brought up with Christian ideals, the feeling is one of disapproval towards divorced and remarried people playing an active part in the church. Linked to this also is the notion that any official support for stepfamilies is an approval of divorce. This attitude is reinforced by governmental authorities too: funding requests for stepfamily support have been turned down with the explanation that this would be seen as an endorsement of family break up. Concern has been strongly voiced at the proposals in the Family Law Bill, currently being debated, to shorten the period before a divorce is made final.

The very word, step-parent, sounds odd and even old-fashioned like something out of a folk tale. Yet everyone knows exactly what it means. My edition (1992) of the Oxford Reference dictionary has a long paragraph about every kind of step including 'step in' to enter or intervene, all of which could be recognized as descriptive, if not desirable. Of step, as in people, it has this to say: 'prefix denoting a relationship like the one specified (stepfather, stepmother, stepsister, stepbrother) but resulting from a parent's remarriage.' The entry also has the language origins of step. The word is from Old English, related to Old High German, and the original meaning is given as 'bereave' and, in

Chambers dictionary, as 'orphan'. Accordingly, therefore, a step-parent is a parent through bereavement rather than birth. Knowing this original meaning could make the vivid folk tales of stepfamilies – notably Snow White and Cinderella – more about the cruel suffering of loss and grieving for the child rather than the cruelty of the actual stepmother. The feelings of being alone, abandoned, unprotected and, as were the old customs, being denied the finery and colours of clothes associated with a normal, happy family life was the stepchild's lot. Cinderella's rags and the cinders of her name and duties, reflect the sackcloth and ashes of extreme grief, of mourning. However much these ideas and customs have been forgotten or left behind with time there is still sadness when one parent leaves. Even though this sadness may not last, a separation is still a form of bereavement for all concerned. The joyousness of a new love will bring renewed life to the family but if the sadness hasn't been expressed or the bereavement acknowledged the renewal can not really take effect.

Labels And Images

The rational and factual image of a stepfamily is rarely presented. Can you think of any well-known personalities you would associate with a stepfamily? There are plenty of well-known divorces and remarriages, but who is a step-parent or a step-sibling? Part of this is to protect the privacy of the children but more often the fact is just ignored and yet it is such a big experience. Images of children of separated parents as disturbed children has been cultivated by the media and by the use of sociologists' comments. Children whose parents' marriages have ended have been described by 'experts' in newspapers and on television as 'underachievers'. Labels are stuck on when things go wrong. When all is well, they are just people. No-one describes Martin Amis or Jasper Conran as having come from stepfamilies. Underachievers? It is a more complex mix.

The respected child psychologist, Bruno Bettelheim, wrote a book called the *Good Enough Parent* to dispel the image of the perfect parent so many aim for, missing the enjoyment of being humanly imperfect. It is easier to have a picture of what should be rather than what could be. However, the good enough stepfamily is a nameless state, a foggy area, even a blind spot. If we come from a Judeo-Christian background we know that King Herod was Salome's stepfather because they had an extremely dubious relationship. Somewhat dimmer is the knowledge that Jesus and Joseph got along well in a simpler stepfamily lifestyle.

If a word like stepfamily is used in association with something good it acquires status and meaning. It is easier to give a bad name. The word stepfather or stepmother used in reporting crime helps to fix the criminality of that person and underline the aberration of his behaviour. Images used in the popular news-papers have a tremendous power and are mainly used to sensationalize in order to grab attention. Therefore stepfamily becomes an extra description in what is a modern folk tale. 'Sometimes when we were arguing he and the kids would gang up on me and jokingly say, "she's the wicked stepmother" and I hated it. I really felt branded.' It still left an impression, so strong is that old tag of wicked stepmother.

Certain terrible stories are remembered by the public as extreme examples of stepfamilies not working, although abuse and violence can occur in all families: A little girl beaten to death by her stepfather; another little girl shut up behind a partition by parent and step-parent and starved to death; a baby boy's skull fractured; a fifteen-year-old girl murdered when she agreed to testify about sexual abuse. The majority of all acts of violence are by men; by culture and physical strength men are more *able* to be violent. That is not the same as saying all men are more *likely* to be violent than women. Cruelty is available to both sexes as a means of dealing with other people. Cruelty is not only physical but also psychological. The way you talk, look even, can carry either warmth and encouragement or disapproval and humiliation. Those newspaper stories tell of children whose destruction was complete. Violence lends itself easily to the disguise of discipline, religious guidance and moral teaching. All these can be milder forms of abuse that leave no outward signs.

8

Stereotypes

Other stories are more likely to imply, rather than say plainly, that divorce and remarriage is synonymous with bad parents, that 'broken homes' can lead to wild, criminal young people. As if a family, once broken and remade as a stepfamily, must have a few cracks, be flawed. Some will indeed be imperfect just as some first families, with all there supposedly ideal ingredients, are too.

However, the desperate loneliness and vulnerability of those damaged children etches the mind with a warning, a question that pricks the heart with a fear that we may not be so high up the evolutionary scale after all. We fear we may be like the animals which destroy the young of a previous mate to ensure loyalty is to the new order. Animals are varied in their instinctive behaviour and humans have the ability to choose. Some animals love and care for the young, content to take their place as an adult powerful enough, in the best sense of the word, to be chosen to do the most important work of nurturing the future. After all, humans only take a few minutes to conceive the next generation, but years to complete the job.

Expectations

How rapidly are new partners pushed into the parent role? Often this happens just too soon and one reason for this is money. The parent who provides the main home finds that this puts on two adults exploring the possibility of love and living together is all tied up with conventional and the State's expectations. The man earns the money and looks after the mother and children. This expectation is supported by the fact that the pyramid employment pattern remains the most common one i.e. men at the peak and women and minorities lower down the salary scale.

But why should the man be rushed into this parent role for financial reasons when it might be better for everyone that the new adult relationship is separate from the existing one of mother and children? At the present time benefits savings and home economics take precedence. It doesn't fit with ideas of equality or independence but it's back to chattels.

To be looked after and cherished is attractive if it's a choice; it's never really a choice if you have to be dependent. And it's back to the idea that there is a model of family life that has always existed everywhere with only an occasional oddity. Sorry, not true.

However, there are always researchers and social historians who look at patterns of behaviour and development and this includes research into family life. The idea that there are cycles in life is useful to demonstrate that nothing is fixed and that change comes about naturally and inevitably. It may not necessarily be in the way we want, unless we get in there to direct it, and it may take time, but if we stay with it change will take place. So when stepfamily life feels unworkable, it can help to remember that it will not stay at that stage. It is a point in a cycle we can direct.

In every other situation, work, education, learning to drive, a pattern emerges. It's a decision fired by enthusiasm then it is hard work, frustration and finally – if we're still in there – we win through and find we have achieved our aim. We may not be satisfied with the level of our acquired skill or we may feel fantastic with what we have achieved. Our response is related to personality and attitude rather than measurable ability.

'Fortunately, step-parenting is not an item which can be measured strictly. When social trends are evaluated, they are often based on those families who have come to the attention of social services or who have sought help rather than on those who feel good about their family or those who can work things out for themselves.'

Measuring our feelings against these models of development is useful to see what we think and what we recognize. Relationships are so fluid that any basic rules we follow have a mysterious habit of producing exceptions, so looking at change as development and growth is reassuring. Stepfamilies are varied right from the start, from one child to combined families of several children.

In May 1995 STEPFAMILY, the National Stepfamily Association, was able to say, 'For the first time the word "stepfamily" is to go into an English dictionary.' The short entry is now in the latest edition of the Concise Oxford Dictionary and is a basic definition. STEPFAMILY finds 72 varieties.

Psychologist, Patricia Papernow, who specializes in stepfamily dynamics, has identified a stepfamily cycle with seven stages. These are Fantasy, Immersion, Awareness, Mobilization, Action, Contact, Resolution. The last two stages happen when all the secret anxieties, fears and angers have been voiced and expressed in the process of living together. Acceptance and trust have been established to temper the conflicting needs of the couple, the parent and child, the step-parent and child, and siblings. However, since the emotions within stepfamilies are not conveniently synchronized each member of the stepfamily may slip in and out of each stage at different times. But to look at the apparent conflicts from a perspective of cycles can be extremely reassuring and can provide the encouragement to persevere.

So, don't waste your talents on being the goodie, making it up to your poor, wounded spouse or stepchild, to being the real thing after the initial mistake. Each person in a stepfamily has a point of view and a private experience and these will not depend solely on the step-parent or parent. Whatever the family, someone, some-time, will be unhappy or impossible to get on with or just a complete mystery. The step-parent may even come to identify with the one who came before, the absent birth parent.

Stepfamily Cycle

Fantasy
- The love conquers all phase, full of hopes and dreams of instant harmony.
- Tendency to think that everyone shares the same fantasy.

Immersion
- Sink or swim reality: confusion and challenge
- Stepfamilies are different to biological families.

Awareness
- Getting to know the real people: you, partner and children.

- Accepting different bonds within the stepfamily
- Seeing others' points of view

Mobilization
- Confidence to voice differences
- Confidence to make changes

Action
- New, shared decisions based on agreement
- New stepfamily customs emerge
- More realistic bonds with stepchildren
- Supportive of children's contact with other birth parent

Contact
- Confident and established intimacy
- Partners support each other
- Step-parent role becomes clear

Resolution
- Stepfamily flexible, independence within group security
- Step-parent can give advice in sensitive areas e.g. sex, drugs, homework, late nights
- Defined private times for the adult couple

The special situation of the stepfamily is beginning to receive more attention. There are:

- More books and other positive media coverage
- Acknowledgement of financial support for first family
- Acknowledgement of costs of subsequent families
- More self-help groups which take account of stepfamily needs
- National association campaigns which inform and dispel myths

Chapter 2
Stepmothers

At first Aoife felt affection and honour for the children of Lir. Lir doted upon the children and they always slept in beds near their father. But thereupon the dart of jealousy passed into Aoife on account of this and she came to regard the children with hatred and emnity.

The Children of Lir, Celtic Fairy Tales

ALTHOUGH there are now fewer stepmothers than stepfathers, it is a very well-known role from the old stories that children still love to hear.

The stepmother is part of so many folk tales, a popular hate figure. Snow White, Cinderella, the Children of Lir, Vasilisa, all had stepmothers who were decidedly malevolent. In folk tales the stepmother is seen as supplanting the 'real' mother, a rather saintly, dead mother replaced by a false model. The stepmother plays a part in novels, fortunately not always a monster and, in modern literature, she simply reflects the variety of women. The stepmother as stock character, like the mother-in-law, has disappeared in fiction, but remains in our psyche.

Historically, women were very likely to die in childbirth or from puerperal fever or from contagious illnessess like TB. Understanding of the role of hospital hygiene, improved standards of living, antibiotics and the founding of the National Health Service after the Second World War have all contributed to the mother's survival. Before this, however, fathers looked for second wives who would be stepmothers for their children, even where the extended family still existed as relatives often had other children to care for. In the early 20th century, romance became more important, at least as a prelude to marriage as better job prospects and, therefore some independence, changed women's expectations. In the 19th century, when the vision of spinsterhood was one of poverty and of low status in society, it was a far better choice to marry a widower and become a stepmother than to remain single. It was a sensible, even desirable, job for women who did not exactly have many other opportunities, and love was not a prerequisite. After all, conjugal rights were enshrined in law until the 1950s. Men could go to court and apply for a legal ruling to force a wife back to the marital bed. Love was not an absolute essential. Perhaps women had a better or at least more realistic view of what they were taking on. That's not to say they were happier, or morally superior, or produced perfectly balanced young adults and contented couples. It was a different society. We have to deal with what we have now. But it isn't clear what that is just as the circumstances that precede a stepfamily now are often emotionally murky.

Women fall into the role of stepmothers in several ways, through divorce, separation, extra marital affairs and through death, and the tendency is to be, not second best, but a superior model. Competitiveness is tempting when the birth mother is likely to be alive and happily living with someone else. This urge to be better than the original partner does not always fit well with the children's leftover pain and confused feelings. Whatever happened to the children's mother, it is all too easy for the stepmother to want to be more than good enough. She wants to be excellent. Second time round, it has to be good.

GROWING INTO THE STEPMOTHER ROLE
Stepmothers are not necessarily aware that they are trying to prove a point but the role is less spontaneous than becoming a mother, it doesn't grow, it is a ready-made part without any instructions. Although for some becoming a stepmother is a gradual process, thought through and planned jointly, for others the role appears unexpectedly.

Dot did become a stepmother unexpectedly when her partner's ex-wife died. Father and daughter, suffering from shock, moved into her flat and Janey, aged nine, who had been living with her mother, said, 'Can I call you Mummy?'

Dot and Richard already had an established relationship and this was as two equally independent people not a domestic basis. Now, on top of the emotional trauma suffered by both father and daughter, child care and domestic arrangements had to be agreed. It was very hard work. Dot had a demanding job and enjoyed getting back to her own flat and now there were two people in it, needing her. All three were having to make big adjustments to their lifestyle and expectations and they did succeed. That was ten years ago. This year is the first Janey has not joined the adults on holiday. Ten years on, Richard and Dot have two young children and the family home is a house not Dot's bachelor flat.

The issues which this stepmother faced were the sudden and new emotional demands thrust upon her and the decision to be willing to change her life to accommodate her new role. She could have remained independent and given her time and support only until her partner and his child had recovered from their bereavement. After all he could have taken on his daughter and kept his separate relationship with Dot where both worked and lived separately, but the turmoil pushed them into a new stage in their relationship and they went along with this without becoming completely swamped.

The experience changed Dot from an independent and ambitious career woman who felt self-conscious about hugging her unhappy and needy stepdaughter to a woman who had to trust that she wouldn't lose herself by becoming a stepfamily. You could say that as well as finding new resources in herself, she brought her proven professional ability home and used it to cope.

While she needed the rewards of going to work, her husband – they did eventually marry – did have a good salary as a university professor so, rather than return and compete in a narrowing world of employment, she decided, after a few years of adapting to her role as wife and stepmother, that it was the time to have children of her own and work for satisfaction as a voluntary fundraiser. Voluntary organizations are always looking out for people with time and skills and being a fundraiser is no longer an easy option for the privileged dabbler. They have to be good if they represent

15

*the public face of an organization and this can be as exciting and as
demanding as any high-flying job.*

Dot was fortunate to be able to choose. Staying at home is not a choice
for some when there are so few jobs available or jobs that do not pay
enough to make work worthwhile. The balance between staying at
home or going out to work is confused by the poverty trap of
unemployment and benefits. However, it is not only the stepmother
with a well-earning husband who gets a life outside the home.

*Shirley is 30 and has two children and a younger stepdaughter.
Her partner is a self-employed decorator so doesn't always have
regular work. They live in a small maisonette on an old council
estate. She has also done the traditional thing and taken on most
of the child rearing work. Her way of keeping a life of her own is
through adult education courses and going to the local gym.*

*Both stepmothers have in common this determination to keep a
life of their own and they do this by going outside the home. Dot has
the advantage of money and experience and Shirley has the support
of her parents living next door and a good arrangement with the
father of her two children. The stepmothers gained extra confidence
by using and developing their talents and having an independent
social life using the network that is outside the stepfamily.*

Keeping your own life going and drawing on resources outside the
home is harder when there are several children. Stepmothers may
have children at home and others may be visiting all at the same
time so there may be few occasions when the stepmother is not on
demand. The unspoken rule seems to be that if you're there people
will lean on you, gratefully or otherwise.

*Chrissie became a stepmother when she was expecting her first
baby by her partner John. His wife, Lorraine, arrived from the
Scottish island where she was living also pregnant by John.
Chrissie knew about Lorraine but she was far enough away to
be out of sight, out of mind. Lorraine and John had parted on
friendly terms and she had asked if he would look after their*

two little girls, two and a half and three and a half, while she organized her return to London.

John, being a laid-back aspiring rock musician said, 'Sure' and told Chrissie his children were arriving to stay and needed looking after. Chrissie didn't feel she could refuse. 'I didn't know anything about children and I felt very shy of these little girls. They looked so beautiful and colourful, dressed in clothes their mother had made. I just felt terrified.

When Lorraine left them John said, 'Why don't you take Sharon out in the garden' and I was relieved to have something obvious to do which was to give her a go on the swing. I gave a big push and she immediately fell off. It did improve but after living in the country in such a remote place they were completely wild and not at all shy about saying things like 'I'm going to make the bunk bed fall on your head.'

Chrissie had once been a secretary, she then went to Glastonbury, dropped out and met John while doing street theatre. John was a musician and lived in a communal house. This wasn't a recipe for alternative poverty. John also had a very successful small business. By the time he was 28 and Chrissie was 26, they had five children, three of whom were Chrissie's stepchildren and two from their relationship. It was then, according to Chrissie, that traditional roles reappeared. She stayed at home with the children; he worked and spent the evenings down at the pub. Inevitably, the children dominated Chrissie's time, energy and love. Being immersed in five demanding relationships there was not much time and energy left over for the adult who, however good at earning an income, arrived home round midnight.

The point of this story is that in spite of the overwhelming hard work and, in the end the break-up of the family, Chrissie and the children did stay in touch, did talk, did see each other as a family. There were so many needs in this ready-made family, overlapping with new additions that there was no time left over to take stock and see what was happening. Neither was there breathing space for the adults to see how they wanted the future to unfold. Chrissie slipped into taking on all responsibility for *the children, neglecting her own needs for love, support, attention and practical help.*

Being an excellent stepmother can result in forgetting the one you wanted to be with in the first place. Do you identify with any of this? It can also mean giving up your own aspirations; that was certainly the end of street theatre for Chrissie, swopped for home drama. It isn't unusual to be in one sort of family and find it transformed into something you did not originally have in mind.

Coping And Sharing

Shirley had put a lot into keeping a good friendship with the father of her two children, Natalie, 14, and Fitz, 8, and they stay with him every weekend. This ideal had been forged out of goodwill, Shirley's perseverance and Natalie's strong attachment to her father. He tended to turn up late, was a bit of a streetwise man. So she had done well to keep the family in touch, if not intact, and her boyfriend, Barnes, had become the man in her's and Fitz's life.

However, four years into this stepfamily Shirley's visiting stepdaughter, Kaysha, came to stay. 'Just like that,' *she explained,* 'I can't understand how her mother can do that. She hasn't thought about her daughter or anyone else. It is very hard for me to like Kaysha as I hadn't any choice. I've lost my weekends as now I've got to look after her when my children are away.'

Her anger is with the child's mother and to some extent, her boyfriend because Kaysha is their child and yet Shirley, the stepmother, finds herself doing their job of child rearing. No wonder she also finds it hard to like Kaysha, describing her as a bit sneaky. 'As far as coping goes I find if I bend over too much she takes advantage or if I resort to getting angry it means I haven't got through to her and then I blame myself. I have Natalie coming to me, complaining she touches her things. Natalie always had her own room and now she has to share.'

In a three bedroom home where do you make a place for a five-year-old stepdaughter when there are already two children, a girl of fourteen and a boy of eight? The first time I talked with Shirley for this book she had forgotten our date and was in her dressing gown, and soon tears just rolled down her cheeks. And this is a woman everyone knows as feisty and capable, never afraid to speak her mind. When you have a good, strong self-image it is easy to forget that in some circumstances you will not always be strong. Although young, Shirley had recurring infections after a hysterectomy and was feeling pretty low after yet another hospital visit.

The second time I visited, Shirley was her usual bright self. 'I was feeling so down and had stopped doing any of my own things. Anyway I did say something.' she smiles, 'either Kaysha's mother took her at the weekends or else Barnes had to. He's her father and he's not working at the moment.' Shirley is back at college too, and she has been able to restore the balance. Maybe putting it into words and having a cry helped to bring home the truth that it was too much. I can't help thinking also of the other elements in Shirley's role as a mother and, although they are unique to her, I believe we all have our versions. She related how distressed she was, as a young girl, when her mother sent a younger sister to live with a relative. This was the child Shirley had loved and had mothered, *'I felt she had no right to send her away from me.'* When the younger sister was a teenager she eventually came to live with Shirley in her own home, so there is a very powerful background of looking after other children, of taking on a mothering role early in her life. The present situation was made less bearable because of the pattern that had come before.

WHEN STEPMOTHERS DIVORCE

Chrissie was the stepmother who loved too much and lost herself and her husband in the process. The children, half-sisters, thrived and remain close to each other and the three stepdaughters eventually forged a new relationship with Chrissie, one where she doesn't feel over-responsible and doesn't compare herself to any past or current mother. It's a friendly, caring relationship with the girls visiting her and their half-siblings. She may not be married to John any longer but she is still part of the family and will always be. Children do not divorce each other.

One story that comes back to me now, although I heard it several years ago, was that of Kay who bumped into her stepson in the street. After the initial awkwardness they started chatting and she went on her way spirits lifted by the unexpected pleasure of the short, surprise conversation. She knew then that her relationship with the boy had not been erased from his mind. Her ex-partner had not wanted his son to stay in touch with her and she had felt bitter at being excluded from a relationship with the 12-year-old boy that had ended by a decision that neither she nor the boy had made. Both Chrissie and Kay had become ex-wives but had very different experiences in their relationship with the stepchildren after their marriages had broken up.

Marlene is in her forties and has been with her man, Glen, since she was nearly fifteen, he is a year older. If Chrissie was the stepmother who loved too much then Marilyn is married to a classic figure who fortunately has – I hope – gone out of fashion; the man who loves too much. 'He is a real Casanova,' she tells me and I understand how he earned that title when I hear that he has eight children to prove it. Marlene and Glen have two children together and she has acquired several of the other six as stepchildren.

'He is very much in touch with all of the children. When we went on holiday this summer one stepdaughter and a stepson came with us and our two children. I get on well with them especially as my stepdaughter is good friends with mine. No-one would think that Joscelyn and Dion were from different mothers. Dion asks for my advice, you would think she was my child.'

The son, Lascelles, (by another mother) spends every weekend at Glen and Marlene's home and she believes in creating a welcoming place for her husband's children. It hasn't been easy. 'I was too soft, too easygoing with his unfaithfulness towards our relationship,' *she says,* 'then I suddenly woke up out of that dream and took a good look at myself and my family. My mother and my sister made me aware of what I was doing.'

She gave Glen an ultimatum and they had a four-year break. 'And that's when he lived with Lascelle's mother. He still visited our children and, after the other relationship didn't work out, he edged his way back in. But I said no, and this time

I told him what I expected if we got back together. He is much more mature since we had that gap.'

In spite of the many years of hurt and betrayed feelings caused by Glen's affairs, Marlene enjoys her stepchildren and does appreciate the pride Glen takes in his children. He isn't an absent parent but keeps in touch with them all and that's accepted by Marlene as she sees the benefit of friendly behaviour towards all the children, including her own. 'If there's a family party or a wedding all his children will come. They all phone and talk to their father and that's fine.'

What is noticeable is that the children are labelled as 'his children' and some are 'you'd think she was my child'. Literally caring for a child, spending time with them in the home, going on holiday, listening to the mother on the phone regarding the child's health, all these make a husband's child your stepchild. The good friendship between the sisters and the obvious affection and care by Glen for all the children make it possible for Marlene to accept and love them. Some of the other mothers see Marlene as an obstacle and do not want any contact with her and, while Glen has some parental role in the children's lives, including telephone calls, Marlene doesn't. There's no doubt that the moment when Marlene said no to Glen's behaviour she began to regain some measure of power in her house. She could then choose her situation rather than be burdened by it.

PARALLEL FAMILIES

This way of becoming a stepmother is not as rare as you may think. Yes, there are men who have parallel families and men who scatter children but do not acknowledge or keep in touch with them. In spite of the largely faded images of the Casanova, the bohemian and the bigamist, there are still a few around.

Some of these men rather enjoy their offspring coming home to roost. Perhaps they think once wife and stepchild have met, like Marlene and Dion, all will be forgiven or that the child, once met, could never be rejected.

Other situations exist where the emotions and loyalties are more complex. Where husband, wife and mistress and children agree, even if unwillingly, or implicitly accept, that a separation and a remarriage is not the right answer for all concerned. That this situation is not rare, unusual perhaps, is borne out by the occasional newspaper story (usually about a politician) of a man with two co-existing families.

GOOD MOTHERING AND GUILT

The powerful imprint of the always loving mother handed down through religion and culture is carried over into stepmotherhood. For some this is Mary and Jesus; for others the famous Jewish Mamma, the bountiful provider of nourishment. There are many versions of 'the angel at the hearth'. Freud took this and turned the picture of the self-sacrificing mother round to represent some of the stifling aspects of family life from which the children later had to extricate themselves from by a second cutting of the umbilical cord. The stiflingly good mother became an obstacle to the children's development.

In post-war modern psychology, the mother who went out to work, was considered to be the cause of many problems. The 'latch key kid' was the ultimate deprived child. Add on the cruel, jealous stepmother and it's a no-win situation. How can any woman rise above all this? If you're good, you're bad for them, if you're bad, you're wicked.

The earliest known version of this need to blame the woman seems to be our ancestress, Eve, who was conveniently blamed for the suffering of her family and all subsequent descendants thereafter. The latest variation in this blame game is that we as mothers and stepmothers are to aspire to give 'unconditional love' to our children. So it's back to saintliness.

Coping With Negative Emotions

- Take guilt feelings seriously
- Find a 'safe' person to talk to
- Use a helpline or ask your G.P. about counselling
- Don't blame yourself or others
- Move back in situations that spark the 'not good enough' feeling

- Knowing the roots of your own guilt and anger will free you to move into the future seeing yourself and each person in the stepfamily with understanding.

Marian was not a saint and her perceived imperfections caused her much grief. First, she experienced tremendous guilt over the break up of her first marriage through her affair and subsequent remarriage. This guilt caused bouts of depression and then was expressed by fits of uncontrollable rage when plates were smashed. It was hard for her to understand the reason when she also felt love and appreciated the security of a comfortable two-income household. Tension was added through jealousy of the close relationship between her husband and his daughter, Annabel.

'They would be holding hands, he is a very physical person with his own children. I just felt jealous there's no other word for it. They are so spontaneous and easy together. Annabel has cystic fibrosis and needs care so I have to be even more careful not to show my feelings.'

Sometimes two causes of frightening feelings add up, making each separate feeling worse. Marian does talk to her husband about her feelings and copes by reminding herself of all the times she has without the two stepchildren and the times she has as a couple without children or stepchildren. Her practical moves to ensure they all get to have times with parent alone reduces what the fairy story calls so tellingly 'the dart of jealousy'.

None of us are indispensable. We don't have to be a stepmother all the time. Leaving the family for a few hours or a few days is refreshing. Shirley's dilemma was left on hold while she was a student at college, maintaining a life of her own made a difference to her and consequently the stepfamily. However much we are committed to our family and however much we share parenting with the man of the home, it does not mean we have to be there all the time.

Positive Attributes A Stepmother Can Bring

- Fresh attitudes to family customs
- Ideas on helpful, practical changes

- Source of advice and understanding for stepdaughters at puberty.
- A more detached view on sensitive subjects e.g. sex, drugs, late nights
- Mentor for shared or special interests

Stepmother Strategies

- Begin with friendship
- Avoid trying to replace the mother
- Accept child's need for photos and other signs of the mother
- Accept contact with mother
- Allow the child one-to-one time with Dad
- Avoid criticizing or ignoring the mother's gifts
- Be clear about what you want but not demanding
- Keep a life of your own

Checklist

- Who is your competitor for his affection/attention?
- What have you stopped doing that you used to enjoy?
- Do you have a space that is yours, however small?
- Is the home formerly yours, his or is it a new territory?
- Do you find yourself doing more and more of the childcare?
- How often do the children stay with their mother?
- Who agrees the arrangements?
- Who reads bedtime stories, you the stepmother or their father?
- Who goes to parent evenings? Both of you? Him?
- Is he working so hard and such long hours that you haven't the heart to ask for help with the children?
- What, in an ideal world, would you ask him to take over?

Chapter 3
Stepfathers

Gradually, I became used to seeing the gentleman with the black whiskers. I liked him no better than at first, and had the same uneasy jealousy of him; but if I had any reason for it beyond a child's instinctive dislike, and a general idea that Peggotty and I could make much of my mother without any help, it certainly was not *the* reason that I might have found if I had been older.

David Copperfield, by Charles Dickens

T HE MODERN man is expected to play a part in the home, helping with the daily routine of care for the children, cooking and other domestic demands. When these children are not his own but have had a life without him and he a life without them how does he manage in this newly-formed unit? What is the special quality required for being a stepfather? Even in these modern times when both men and women work and aspire for equality in the home, the stepfather's role is different. Whether through nature or by nurture, women are expected to provide cuddles to the younger children and warm understanding to older ones. A stepfather, especially if he doesn't have children living in the stepfamily, is associated with giving support to the mother and, through her, to the children. As an eldest daughter assured her mother, 'When you're happy then I'm OK too' He is seen as helping to create a stable and, perhaps, more financially secure home and completing that socially desirable unit of dad, mum and children.

Some of those images may be views from the outside, may be considered stereotypes, but most single parents want to have another adult as part of their lives sharing the work of creating and sustaining a harmonious household.

JOINING THE FAMILY

A stepfather comes into a close unit of mother and child or children. If they have been happily living together without a man in the family, the children may question the need for change. If the emotions have been volatile and upsetting in the family, then why tempt fate again a second time with a stepdad? What has he got to offer? As long as the mother's new relationship stays mainly outside the home boundaries he may be a much appreciated family friend. However, once the decision has been made for him to move into the family home he must work for a rightful place and this may not be an easy task. The mother may lack a man and may want a husband but the children do not lack a father even if he is not there in the home every day. He exists as part of them and, whether they love him or hate him, he is carried around in some part of their memory. Loyalty to the father and even a protectiveness towards him may cause a certain reserve towards the stepfather – 'Does this man want to replace our Dad for us too?' Children are not blinded by love and may see some very clear signs of trouble lurking beneath the surface. What a stepfather or prospective stepfather says and does when the child is there, is remembered and thought about. Children do notice what is going on even when they do not understand. A girl sees her prospective stepfather chatting up another woman and behaving in a way that seems at odds with their new family life, although she would not say exactly why she held certain emotions against him until she became an adult.

However, the stepfathering only really begins when a joint home is set up. As Ray and Carol found out:

Ray married Carol and moved into her house. He really did things by the book. Friendship came first and he didn't stay the night. Carol told her daughters and son if she ever had a new man in her life she would tell them. They would never find a strange man in her bed as had happened to a friend of her daughter, Becky; so mother and children had a good and frank talk.

Children may not appear to notice that parents have a sexual life together but, once the partner is someone else, not a parent but a step-parent then you know they know. The stepchild has lost one parent and now has that role fulfilled by an outsider, a nice, good person doubtless, but someone who has a unique intimacy with Mum.

As a straight talking, hard working man Ray believed in doing the right thing and giving a good example: 'I took things slowly. Carol said she wanted to do things a certain way and I believed she was right, I admired the fact she thought about the kids. I was around for quite a few months before I'd stay overnight.'

So the relationship moved from being friends to being a couple without Ray actually moving in. He talked over getting married with Carol and waited for her to bring it up with her children. He believed this would show the children, hers and his own, that he cared about them and Carol, that his intentions were honourable, as they say. He wanted to prove his commitment.

However, the years with him as stepfather have been quite a battle. The girls resented Ray, and expressed it freely, in spite of both adults preparing the way with such care: 'After the years of "You're not my father" and the arguing, I believe we now think the world of each other, so the effort to keep going has been worth it,' *Ray explained.*

The girls were close to their mother and used to her style of family agreements and fought against changes. Conversely, Ray and stepson, Dave, got on brilliantly. That was ten years ago and the stepchildren have almost left the nest. The two girls are now at college and travelling in the long holidays, the boy is at home. Their relationship with Ray was fine while he remained a family friend, outside their home boundary, but the moment Carol told them: 'From now on Ray's going to be sleeping in my bed on Saturdays', *they resented his presence, his ideas about how things should be done, resented him moving into their family home:* 'It's not exactly calm now but it works,' *he says.*

Avoiding Conflict

Different standards apply to new members of an established family. A child may look and compare the new person to Daddy or an idealized Daddy. We all have faults and opinions and the stepfather may find that however charming, human and fascinating these attributes may be to the mother, they can be seized upon and mercilessly examined by a stepchild of any age except, of course, the tiny baby. Naturally, this can be infuriating to say the least, and no amount of justification or explanation will soften their attitude. Strategies devised by the adults need to be subtle, even if the child's attacks are not, and confrontations only confirm the fact that there is a battle.

Tony and Marian live in his house with her two children, his stepdaughter and stepson. 'Occasionally I'll wind my step-daughter up by chatting about fox hunting. She is very into animal rights and a vegetarian and I do find her very irritating, but mostly I make an effort to avoid creating tension and since the main meal is the likely time for friction Marian and I eat later.'

It isn't surprising that Tony still feels his own son and daughter from his first marriage are visitors in the house they used to live in but he gets round the conflict of meeting everyone's needs by spending some time just with his own children when they stay. He also feels it is acceptable to keep in the background sometimes and not try to be everything for everyone. All the four children are in their teens, old enough to have independent relationships with their birth father and birth mother and therefore do not need a surrogate parent or need to spend as much time in the stepfamily group which suits Tony.

His main motivation is to be with Marian and the harmony of the stepfamily is important to support that adult relationship. Naturally, he wants the stepchildren to feel at home and

*to feel good about their new family, but he does not demand
that he is as important as their natural parent. For Tony, being
a stepfather does not mean being in that role all of the time.*

I was surprised (and a touch relieved) to find that friction
between stepfathers and stepdaughters is quite common. This area
of conflict is normal and, as Ray's experience demonstrates,
possible to overcome. When you have identified the ingredients
for potential conflict in your stepfamily and you realize that they
exist in other stepfamilies, you can at least look for strategies,
rather than blame yourself or look for someone else to blame.

Common Ingredients of Conflict

- Eldest daughter
- Jealousy that role as mum's friend and companion is
  usurped
- Loyalty to natural father
- Secret hope of parents' reunion
- Resentment at moving home or other changes
- Convenient newcomer to dump on

Tony's Strategies

- Change the situation where arguments happen e.g.
  avoid eating together every evening
- My children visit often which makes me feel more
  relaxed
- I have a week on holiday alone with them.
- This lessens the impact of niggling friction on my
  children.
- Don't completely ignore difficult subjects
- Don't forget to give compliments when due
- Be genuine, you're not perfect

Even the reverse, where the prospect of a stepfather is a source of
delight, may lead to problems. A single mother may be disturbed by
unforeseen emotions, feeling she is no longer head of the family, the
one who makes decisions and creates the home atmosphere.

Territory – feeling at home

The new man does not just walk in off the street into the home. Although it is sensible to pace moving in together, it does not always make it any easier in practice. Then there's the question of whether the stepfather joins the ready-made family, or do they all uproot and share his territory, or are both adults able to overcome the two upheavals of moving and getting a new place together? More often than not there isn't a choice. Peter, a stepfather, thinks it is essential to make a new start on neutral territory without complicated memories and it took a few years (while he lived in his wife and stepchildren's home) until they could do that. Ray moved in with Carol and says he still feels, ten years on, that he's on Carol's territory. Both Peter and Ray are also fathers and are accustomed to a family home where they had an equal part in setting it up.

What sort of stepfathers are there anyway? Parent substitute, friend, playmate, uncle figure – do you remember that euphemism? Most children knew there was something odd about a man they had to call uncle. Maybe that has disappeared from popular use now. Adults can divorce and remarry and do not have to disguise the nature of their relationship but, for those with a Catholic background, particularly from an Irish Catholic family, this has been very difficult. The 'Yes' vote in the 1995 divorce referendum in the Irish Republic is only the beginning of a change of heart in Irish society. Separation can bring embarrassment for the rest of the family and this can be a powerful deterrent to a partner openly enjoying a new relationship where the children will benefit too.

Friend Or Father Figure

Can a stepfather be a friend and step back from any hint of a replacement father? Is it more honest and practical that a stepfather takes on an openly responsible role showing the children that he is a partner in every sense. Age, both of step father and step children, makes a difference. 'When I'm being realistic I know it's bound to be a process. I am very conscious that she is a girl who's nearly a woman. That's one of the strains of having a stepdaughter who was old enough not to accept me, and to be fiercely loyal to her father. And we don't have anything to talk about naturally as our sets of interests are so far apart. Even so, I try to be interested in her which is easier now she's at college. Studying is something I understand about.' So speaks Michael, a man of 38 about a young woman of 17.

Joe's adopted (ex-step) daughter is 13, a big girl for her age, says Joe, who at, 30, is clearly a little young to be her father: 'I still have a slight feeling of embarrassment when Lily comes down to the courts with me – I'm a tennis coach – I wish I didn't feel compelled to explain but I do.' When the child is young it may be easier for the stepfather to be accepted as a parent figure even where the birth father has an active part in the child's life. The younger the child, the more likely to want to say 'Daddy' to the man who does the day-by-day fathering.

Stepdad or dad

Some stepfathers arrive on the scene so early in a child's life that it is not possible or sensible to be anything other than a parent and, at some stage, the parents will have to decide how to explain the fact that he is not the birth father. It is better to explore how to do this well in advance. If this is not tackled between the couple, it will lead to a dilemma later because the child will eventually find out the truth. When Steve met his partner a baby was already on the way, the child is now nine years old and is still not aware that his 'father' is a step father.

Jason met his wife when he came to Britain on an extended holiday from St Lucia. When Yvonne realized that she was pregnant, she did not want to have an abortion. Jason had come to visit relatives living in this country and to have a break before taking up a job back home, his best opportunity yet. Instead, he found himself making the decision to stay, get married and become a father and stepfather in the space of four months. His son is three months old, his stepdaughter is 18 months.

'My son is her brother and they will grow up in a family together. How we'll tell her I can't imagine now. A lot depends on her father if he suddenly wants to see her. I'm too gobsmacked at all that's happened. Happy, but gobsmacked. In a way being pushed into a family so rapidly has made me feel more responsible than I would have ever thought possible.'

In some families, the children know the facts and are able to choose. In Mark's family the younger children say 'Dad', knowing he is indeed a stepfather, and the older ones do not call him dad, but by his first name, Mark. A young child who does not have so much family history, not so many memories and customs, will have more need for someone to be there most of the time, picking up and holding, kissing and hugging. Calling that person 'Dad' fits in with being conventional and 'normal' at primary school among his peers.

In Catherine Cookson's story of a widow who remarries, it takes some time before the children want him to be dad and, even then, however much the trials of stepfamily life are romanticized, the children have different titles for his different roles.

> It was odd, she thought, how her four children,
> including Mamie her adopted daughter of five,
> would all revert to the name of Mr Bill when
> they wanted him to champion them. It was only
> since the Christmas before last, months after
> she and Bill had been married, that they had given
> him the title of Dad.
>
> from *Bill Bailey's Lot* by Catherine Cookson

Competition

It is easy to assume that the younger the child the more accepting of a new man as a father figure, however the opposite can be equally true. The openly competitive nature of a small child may make him resent an outsider taking up the time and attention of the parent. The child of a single parent is accustomed to a one-to-one relationship even if the father helps to bring up the child. As they are not living together, each parent is more likely to spend separate time with the child. When another adult male moves in on the scene a small child immediately responds either with jealousy or with friendliness. Sometimes an a child remains unbearably needy even when effort has been made to please, spend time, entertain and be attentive. A stepfather, whatever the age of the children, naturally moves on from this role to the one where he does not feel a need to prove himself, where he can be himself, warts and all. This, too, has a good and a bad side.

> *Paul rushed in and wanted to make everything all right for his two stepchildren who were then nine and seven years old:* 'It's a natural human impulse to want to improve things, I think. Anyway I steamed in and said "we're going to do things this way" which was a bit of a mistake. Lots of attitudes and ways of doing things are set by then and now I often agree to disagree if it's not my way of doing things. Change is slow and I've come to realize I need to be more accepting of the children as they are. The older the stepchild, the harder it is to work these things out.'
>
> *There are still tensions between Paul and his stepdaughter, the eldest child who at 12 is just moving into puberty with all its attendant emotional turmoil. He tries hard, perhaps too hard, and the feeling is all too often of underlying friction.*

In theory, it may seem strange that a grown man should feel at the mercy of a child but this is not uncommon. Sincere and kind efforts towards a stepdaughter who is simmering with resentment can be rejected and challenged as if to say, 'OK go on prove yourself to me, see if you can win my affections'. All that happens is both effort and failure fix the two more firmly in a terrible unspoken battle.

A man with good intentions of creating a happy stepfamily has a problem understanding what on earth he can do when, although the adult, he seems to be the powerless one. Also it is often one child who seems to intensify the difficulties and divided loyalties. An eldest child – and it is most likely that friction will exist between stepfather and the eldest child – will act out a mix of adult responsibility and childish anger.

A New Baby

The most affectionate and stable relations between stepfather and child can be disturbed when a new baby arrives. Joe and stepdaughter, Lily had become close over two years, he then married Lily's Mum, adopted Lily and, soon after, baby Emma was born.

'Lily has changed a lot from a quiet, even sad, girl of eight to a much happier and more confident girl. She is very pleased at having the same name as us, but it was difficult for her when Emma came along. When Emma was born I had an instant fatherly bond and that bond is different between me and Lily. We do talk about it and she's very wise.'

The new baby syndrome can affect a stepfather and son just as much as it did Lily and Joe. The arrival of a child that is not a stepchild throws the identity that was secured into doubt all over again. Someone has come between child and mother once already, then along comes 'their' child.

Sean was 13, the stepfamily had been established for eight years but the birth of a sister threw all his hard-won confidence in both adults into doubt. The behaviour that expresses jealousy is often very unattractive and upsetting to the adults who are immersed with feelings of tenderness for this small, new, family member and who is a tangible expression of their love.

Sean loves his sister now but it was a shock to him as well as the rest of the stepfamily when he reacted so strongly. Stepfather, Simon, talked it over with his wife and left some space for mother and eldest child.

'It wasn't easy to see Veronica at the mercy of two demanding children. The alternative was an adolescent freaking out. My son, Brian visits and although Sean and Brian aren't great friends that hasn't been nearly such a strain and my son isn't a bit jealous of the baby. I don't understand it at all but boy did this baby cause an upset here.'

There are hiccups to the most harmonious stepfamilies at times and these are not easily predictable. On holiday, when mother and stepfather want to spend a bit of adult time together the happiest stepchild can become demanding and interfering.

Competition
- Accept there are moments when parent and child need time alone
- Find a co-operative activity
  cooking or other practical task with instant results
- Make appreciative comments
- Take the opportunity for an hour or so to yourself
- Say you know what it is like to be jealous
- Take it slowly and vary effort with spontaneity

Creating a Bond

Robert wants his two stepchildren to spend more time in the stepfamily, (there is a baby in the new relationship) and therefore less time with their father. He sees this as a way of creating a new atmosphere where the loyalty conflict is resolved by making a strong, new, home identity. No doubt spending time together does cultivate a connection and taking trouble over creating a bond is essential and brings rewards but, when good intentions are imposed, they may prove too much for the child to cope with. Many times I have listened to stepfathers talking about their attempts to create a bond, usually by taking a special interest, by going out of their way to be helpful or by buying, sometimes expensive, gifts. I have seen a stepfather buy a camera for a fourteen-year-old with the idea that he could teach her about taking photographs and another who bought his stepchild a model-making kit which was beyond her years. In giving these gifts the stepdad may have been unconscious of his desire to be accepted and to impart some of his happiness into the adult-child relationship. But he suffered from a blind spot about the child. Gifts that are designed for doing something together are a big expectation for the child to live up to, and it may be a real drag for the child to put aside more mundane interests and precious

35

time free from homework and family demands to fulfil these expectations.

Even if the stepfather had said: 'I want to get you something special, something you want for your birthday or Christmas,' there is no guarantee that by producing the desired gift it is going to be fallen on with cries of gratitude. The present may be ignored in spite of careful planning.

Children need time to adapt and may appear unresponsive. They know already that adults are not consistent. Hidden conflicts arise when a stepfather's present is bigger or better than the one from their father. Giving may spring from a desire to show you care but there is an element of display and demand for approval. 'I made such an effort to pay her attention,' mused Chris, 'really treated her as a young woman. She needed shoes and I bought her ones that were smart, fine for school but with a little heel and when I got home my wife looked so disapproving. She didn't say anything in front of Linda who was 12 years old but later on she said they were too grown-up and that it was her job to go shopping with Linda. I felt like I'd done something wrong, almost as if she was jealous.'

If these experiences sound negative and discouraging, Ray did win through and the good relationships will remain when his stepchildren have left home. Family bonds are powerful and past experiences remain as active parts of the present. Ray had some very good comments to make on stepfather sensitivity. One of the most touching was about feeling left out when he had done so much to win his place through hard graft. There is no other word for it, he had really worked at being a stepfather and had overcome many obstacles. 'Like when Becky rang last night from Australia and Carol didn't mention me or pass the phone over. That hurt.' So what else does Ray say about being a stepfather his way? He believes in treating all the children equally, including his own, who live with their mother. He says this is appreciated; he is a practical man and equality includes helping with buying and maintaining a second hand car as each child reaches eighteen years old.

Ray can give the young adult in his care certain things that they want but cannot do for themselves. He is very definite and outspoken about what he expects – namely, they must save up and then he will help. Ray is very clear about what sort of person he is and this is evident to everybody in the family. They do not always like it, but it is not based on their behaviour but on his beliefs. Sometimes this means he does not see the others' points of view.

Ray's Good Stepdad Guide
- Support the children through all their problems
- Treat them equally e.g. presents, household help
- Say what you expect from them e.g. contribution to a major purchase
- Give visible help e.g. be willing to collect them late at night

Many stepfathers talked about having an easygoing bond of common interests. 'I do karate with my stepson and with my son, it isn't a rigid must as they aren't always there but we have done that for years and I enjoy it.' Patrick is faintly surprised that as a quiet and indoor type, he has ended up enjoying a form of sport. Strictly speaking karate is more than that, as any practitioner will explain, and for those who hate the cold outdoors and competition this type of sport could be ideal.

Patrick continues, 'between fifteen and seventeen years of age Simon made it plain that he wanted me to spend time with him, go to a film or wanted to go for a drink with me. Now he's twenty that's stopped although I'm sure if he needed it he would make it happen. I'm not very good at social things but I have learnt to be sensitive to needs flying around.'

If all this sounds very masculine it simply shows there are ways of being together that suit step-parent and stepson. It could just as well be cooking but there is something about being out of the house too, away from the family centre and seeing each other as two adults. Sport is high on the list for going out and escaping the, at times, intensity of home life. Often there is an unspoken understanding when enthusiasms are shared. No-one needs to talk, it is relationship through action and no-one is going to a football match because it is a good idea, but because they love it.

Sport has a lot to answer for though. For every child who supports their team or loves to rush about in one, there is a child for whom fresh air and groups are to be avoided like the plague. The same goes for horseplay and teasing. For some men physical play is communication and for some children it is a form of adult attack. The brave stepdad knows the difference and leaves well alone.

Intimacy And Boundaries

How do stepfathers deal with outside scepticism which ranges from seeing them as some kind of incipient pervert with dubious sexual inclinations or a latter-day rescuer, a romantic fool. In the last decade the abuse of children within the family has received much media coverage. However, along with awareness has come fears of false accusation. A stepfather could only describe his feelings for his stepdaughter as he noticed her growing into a woman. 'I am too young to be her father and I was afraid sometimes, not of what I might do but of how my awkwardness might be interpreted. It's disturbing because she is unselfconscious but I'm not. I don't want anyone who doesn't know us well to read anything into my closeness with her. I'm glad she's left home.'

The percentage of stepfathers responsible for sexual and physical abuse is very small, but there are many other indirect ways of paying attention to a child that are harmful. Concentrating on the 'naughty' child, or overdoing looking for their approval or flirting and teasing however mild, all these can be upsetting even disturbing to the child.

When a man marries a woman who already has children from a previous relationships, his parents may see their dear son either as a knight, or one who is being exploited. They may still think they know what is best for their son despite his maturity. Mark's parents were concerned his romance would prove foolish. 'I had to resist the family misgivings, "Was I taking on far too much becoming stepfather to four children" and there were some disapproving voices in the church.' Vicars as stepfathers are still uncommon but, as Mark says, 'This is modern life and so many parishioners started coming out with their own step relationships, either they had a step-parent or were a step-grandparent and I felt a lot of support.'

Like anything if there is a positive role model from those who have a public profile then everyone gets a confidence boost and will be proud of their chosen family.

Mark's Good Stepdad Guide
- Include the stepchildren in family plans
- Include the stepchildren in wedding plans
- Take a honeymoon later
- Be patient
- Don't impose your past customs e.g. at Christmas
- Don't expect a child to love you instantly
- Don't assume you are instantly strong enough

Stepfathers come in all shapes and personalities. It is often hard to join a home where the mother and child have lived as a self-contained single parent unit. Older children and, research says, girls from twelve years old, may see no advantage in stepfathers at all. They have their loyalties already. Verbal signs of affection are a more appropriate way of making friends.

What a Stepfather Can Offer
- A companion for stepsons with advice during adolescence
- Alternative role model
- May share tastes and interests with stepson or daughter
- e.g. art, football, cooking, bike mending, music
- Releases child from confidant role
- Relieves children from adult discussions and anxieties e.g. finances, work
- Chance to create new home rules
- Fresh approach to old mother and child arguments

Common Step Traps

- Too strict too early on
- Impose new rules too quickly on household jobs
- Jealousy of partner's child
- Too much control
- Not enough consultation
- Not enough tolerance of different customs
- Invasion of child's private areas
- Spoken or unspoken criticism of child's birth parent
- Not understanding child's need to talk about their mum or dad
- Belief that it's better for child not to see birth parent

Chapter 4
Combined Families

With all the permutations of parents, the family is an improbable mix. All the separate members are unconventional in their own ways – which in the past meant all sorts of different signals being given out, and morals that were a maze.

Candida Crewe, *Sunday Mail*, 1995

MY STEPFAMILY was created from two single parents and our five children, later we had a child of our own. We fulfilled one common pattern that even when two sets of children are involved over 50% of stepfamilies have a child in the new relationship. We believed we had common attitudes and interests that would unite us easily, but every so often a chasm of difference would gape between us.

In the early '70s it was unusual for single men to be single parents and provide the main home for their child. When Christopher first moved to the village there was curiosity and approval combined with plenty of women offering help to this paragon. While it was not strictly true that single mothers did not receive help, they, nevertheless, had to create their own network for babysitting and taking children to and from school. Now it is definitely more familiar to see fathers take care of their children both in two parent families and as single parents. Couples may agree this between themselves in a friendly way and courts are increasingly willing to make residence orders (previously known as custody) to fathers. Even so attitudes towards single mothers and single fathers are different. Men who are single parents are praised and supported, at least morally, while women as single parents are stereotyped as undermining the social structure. It is encouraging that these divisions are beginning to soften and merge.

My Family

Holly Young aged 11

There are many issues, and rewards, when two families become one stepfamily. The added combinations of step-siblings and separate customs and different treatment are thrown into the volatile atmosphere of who favours who and the division of territory.

Whose customs are going to survive and whose to change? How can this be sorted out? Is it before or after the big step of sharing a home? Lots of sensible advice on how to prepare or what to say to the children turns out to be impractical because you just do not know all the consequences before you set up home together. *She* didn't know his children got so many presents at Christmas, too many according to her. *He* didn't realize she would keep up her own social life and expect *him* to babysit!

Pat has a son, Jack, 12 and Andy has a daughter, Natasha, 9. They now live together with their children and a child of the stepfamily, Madeline, aged 3. In their two-bedroomed flat in Clapham half-sisters, Natasha and Madeline share a bedroom, while the parents, Andy and Pat, sleep in the sitting-room on a sofa bed and Jack has the treasured asset of a room of his own. I bet he was relieved the new baby was a girl. Space is a big issue when two families live together and this stepfamily take up every inch of theirs. Imagine the demands on the bathroom. So how does each person receive the love and attention that they seek?

Jack was all twelve-year-old irony, 'It was much better before because when it was *just* mum and me we had proper holidays, in Greece.' and Natasha's nine-year-old shyness turned to vociferous opinion. 'Pat's much stricter on me than on him.' *Andy, the family earner, sprawling in a chair after work, offers* 'I've learnt a lot about myself, this . . .' he looks around the small sitting-room full of sofa, armchairs and stepfamily . . . is what I want. It's very fulfilling? *While Pat broke through the hubbub to say with a smile,* 'It has gone much better than I thought it would.' *It seems that one of the disadvantages of being so crowded is that the children interrupt the parents' love life on weekend mornings. Both the children had plenty to say on what it was like since they all lived together and most of it centred on the shortcomings of the adults. In fact they sounded like two old-fashioned parents complaining of untidy bathrooms, neglected household jobs, beery breath and money wasted on frivolous magazines. Any one else sees a couple of adults who are still smiling, who work hard both in and out of the home, who care about their children and the stepfamily and who, after all that, still enjoy life; in short a couple of human beings.*

So how do the parents cope with this onslaught of criticism and individualistic opinion? They listen and offer their own views and the children are encouraged to say what they want to me. The family attitude is that things are better out in the open. Pat was a social worker for fourteen years and has the disadvantage of knowing too much theory and too many statistics, 'We have taken it slowly. We started living together after we had known each other four years, I knew the failure rate for second families is higher than for first families. At least we all knew each other thoroughly. The first thing Jack said to Andy was my boyfriends don't last, that I dump them.'

Before they were married, the distance between Andy's home in London and Pat's in Portsmouth seemed a huge obstacle to a simple love affair, let alone developing a serious relationship with children. This stepfamily shows that there isn't ever an unfailing right way to do things and that there is no reason why single parents should rush in to being stepfamilies. These two visited each other. This way the children's social lives stayed relatively undisturbed and their security wasn't sacrificed to their parents vision of a better future. When the big step did arrive everyone had some idea of what to expect.

THE BIG ISSUES

- Clash of customs and behaviour expectations
- Agreeing a house style of discipline
- Loss of one to one intimacy between parent and child
- Rivalry between the children
- Rivalry between adult and eldest stepchild
- A new baby? Shall we? When?

What is an acceptable level of noise in one home will not be tolerated in another. One child may enjoy quiet hours alone, while another child sees that as strange and is used to being very much in a group. When two single parents get together a big readjustment has to take place but not necessarily all at once. The issues for Andy and Pat did not have to be fully resolved until they had all squeezed into the Clapham flat. The step-parent in each admits the tendency to 'let our own kids get away with murder'; generally Pat is seen as the strict adult while Andy says 'I know how hard Natasha's had it, so for me it's be tolerant and don't be afraid to say sorry'.

Andy is the easygoing one and then, something sparks him off and he loses his temper. Both acknowledge that the children need a certain amount of extra understanding after the insecurity and distress of the past. Both had partners who were involved in drugs and the two children have had more home moves than anyone would choose. It makes a big difference for Pat that Andy understands about being a single parent from experience, 'With other men Jack was a tolerated extra.' Neither Pat nor Andy try to replace the other parent and they value the fact that the children see them. Now that they live together in London, Jack sees his father more often and on a regular basis. However, Jack still likes to look back to the time when it was just him and Pat, when she was working and their standard of living was higher than now – that golden age of holidays in Greece.

Sibling Rivalry

Sibling rivalry is alive and well in this home and it is all out in the open. 'I don't get as much attention now. I'm the eldest and so I get told that I should be an example. I hate it when the bathroom is full of baby's toys all over the place and if I want to watch something on telly and Natasha doesn't then I have to go and watch it in my room.'

Natasha in her turn points out, 'When Jack is bored he wants to play with me otherwise he can be aggressive. I like having a baby sister but Jack throws her toys at me. But sometimes when Pat's out me, my Dad and Jack have pillow fights and share biscuits.' The children agree that if they both want something there is advantage in joint pressure.

The way family arrangements have worked out has led to a certain division of labour. Andy goes to work and Pat stays home with Madeline and does the general looking after the household and organizes family arrangements like a camping holiday in France, which was scorned by Jack.

They have jumped from being a single parent plus one child to a stepfamily of five on a tight budget in a cramped flat. The shared past as single parents brings mutual understanding of the children's need for a reliable contact with their other birth parent. This in turn relieves the pressure and gives the adults some time to pay attention to each other.

Jack's Approved Advantages

- A bigger room
- Now I'm not the only one to blame
- Andy argues with me against my mum
- Have more than one TV
- My own space

Natasha's Approved Advantages

- Pat buys me clothes
- I have a little sister
- Pillow fights
- Pat shows me a tune on her saxophone

Jack and stepsister Natasha have different personalities and characters; they are similar enough in age to be evenly matched in competition although the few years' difference means that they are not at the same school and they are separately interested in a local drama group. They could become more tolerant and friendly to each other, they will certainly gain by it. The increased contact with the other parent gives them all a respite from the demands of a family of five. It is tiring being in a large family after there was only two of you. It is good to get away at times and good to be back.

Andy And Pat's Social life has improved, they go out separately but it is easier to get one babysitter when they go out together. There's shared expenses and, as Andy repeats, 'I know this is what I want. I come from a culture (the Polish community) where large families are common and are a good thing. It's joyful and very fulfilling. And I've learnt a lot about myself.'

Feeling Loved

Many years after growing up in a stepfamily Kathy still feels disappointed that her parents insisted that all the children, her two elder half-sisters and Kathy, should be equally loved. 'I was their child but I was never allowed too much affection in case I was favoured. I didn't want to be loved more than the others, only to know I was loved, just to feel loved.' As an adult Kathy chooses to have very little contact with her older half-sisters. Her comments reflect couples' attempts to be fair and treat all children well. The words 'equally' and 'the same' come up frequently where love is concerned. Is this really honest?

It is hard to find a way that is honest and which does not promote comparison between the children. Naturally, children do not want to hear that one child is loved more than another but there are lots of affirmative, and genuine, statements. 'I love all of you, each one differently' or 'You will always be my first child.' Why not, your own child does need you. Your stepchild also needs his own special love with his parent. And if you are put on the spot, with 'You love me best, don't you?' take that child seriously, but keep what you say simple, plain and not too dreadfully serious. Ask the child about how she loves, and how she loves different people. Remember that this is not an equal conversation, adults and children are not the same, treating children's questions and answers with respect is not treating them as equals. Adults have experience and some wisdom also known as tact!

When nine-year-old daughter, Ruby, asked if her father loved her more than the other children – three stepchildren and a new baby – he replied, mindful of his watchful stepdaughter, that he loved them all, in different ways. 'That was very important to Jaya, too, at 12 the eldest. Prior to that we were two families now I say our family.' He believes this began a fragile bond with his stepdaughter but I wonder if his own daughter was satisfied with his answer.

In stepfamilies with two sets of children there is a tendency for the step-parent to pay more attention to gaining the approval of the stepchildren than that of his own children, where proven love and loyalty already exist. They are a known factor. The stepchild is a key figure, a fierce and critical guardian of the loved one. As Isabel Allende said to her defiant stepson, in Paula, 'We can make an effort and try to love each other, or just treat each other with good manners. Which do you prefer?'

Well meaning attempts at winning approval or being fair to the stepchildren may mean that the parent overlooks his own child's need to know that she, like Kathy, is loved, or like Ruby, needing a reassurance of her special place in her father's heart.

Sibling rivalry has many faces. At times it appears as vying for best loved place with a parent or step-parent, at other times jostling for dominant position among each other at home or in a new social circle. It can manifest itself in teasing, being left out and constant complaining.

Teenage Competition

When the two eldest children are of the same age some clashes are predictable. Marie had a rented flat up the road from Liam's newly bought house. When they met he was converting what had been a stable into a home for himself and his two children. 'This is what my life is like,' he had told her gesturing towards the empty shell. A year later Marie and her two children moved in.

The issues that gradually emerged over the next few years were a different form of sibling rivalry from those experienced in Andy and Pat's stepfamily. The two eldest children attended the same secondary school and were in the same class. Competitiveness at the age of thirteen was compounded by each girl's closeness to her own parent. 'I found I was quite jealous because Katherine was her father's helper,' says Marie, 'and Liam was so used to thinking how wonderful his daughter was and I got sick of hearing him talk about her although I got on with her very well.'

The adults had to watch the challenges the girls set each other which were not always overtly deliberate. Liam's daughter was very academic and surpassed her step-sibling as one of the cleverest girls in the class while Marie's daughter, Lucy, was confident at physical activities but had a long established place in the class both as a capable student and as a popular girl. While the two girls had their difficulties it was not so bad that they could not be friendly. It did stir things up for the respective parent though.

'We don't agree on the amount of freedom the older girls should have. Marie allows the girls to be too grown-up,' *says Liam. However, the growing pangs of teenage girls are a part of any family. The stepfamily group may well have achieved reasonable and comfortable arrangements for all its members, but as the children become older and strive for more independence, the state of that group will change.*

Strategies Summary

- Children adapt slowly
- Explain adult decisions simply
- Respect existing rules or customs
- Make time for one-to-one moments
- Accept parent and child need time together
- Make sure the adults have a respected time or space alone
- Show children you have goodwill towards the other parents
- Give a little and get a little
- Avoid criticizing your new partner in front of or to the children

Sharing Or Independence

One of the exciting aspects of a new stepfamily is the accompanying chance to change. These are not abstract changes but taking on new jobs and relinquishing familiar ones makes you feel different even invigorated. Many practical jobs became easier for Liam and Marie; Liam drove the children to school on the way to work and they shared the cooking and housework. He paid the mortgage and she paid for the weekly shop. They each paid into a joint account.

When one adult owns the family home and the couple are not married then there are questions of equality, decisions and agreements. For example, who owns what? Who has responsibility for maintenance bills? Do unequal earnings all go into a joint account? Marie and Liam had sorted out some of these. But Marie still felt more dependent than she would like. 'At least when I was a single parent I was independent. We do have a better standard of living now. But I can't help thinking, 'Is it alright to spend this?' when I want to buy something for my children. I find that rather than make my own decisions I ask him for advice because he earns more than me and I don't altogether like myself when I do that.'

Both parents are keen supporters of school evenings and attend these together. They are also careful to treat the two girls equally when buying clothes or furnishings for their equally divided bedroom.

Big And Noisy

The good side for the children is that both sets have lots in common, such as pets and music. They enjoy being seen as a big family. Sometimes they like being noisy and chaotic and see themselves as having more freedom in some ways even if the household chores are now organized by rota which feels rather institutional. Space is restrictive for Liam at times, 'When I want to do some work at my desk in the evening I can hear everyone and I want to go and join them. Also I have to have my desk in the bedroom which isn't very big so I've lost the sense of peace and quiet when Katherine would be the only child up. I do look back and I forget that she would have changed anyway, older and more outgoing.'

For another family with two sets of children, five in all, the test of all their faith that living together could work was when one child's cat killed and ate several guinea-pigs belonging to a stepsister. Dad had reinforced the guinea-pig cage and had told his daughter off for neglecting to shut them in securely. When the cat was not being carried around by his doting owner he stared balefully at the attractively large family of guinea-pigs. A massacre in the night set off a family crisis. The cat was sent off to a new home without any discussion. Miraculously this snap decision did not cause a permanent rift between the children, but the cat owner felt no-one was concerned with how she felt. In this home it was pets, in another the clash of interests could be over giving up or having taken away some other precious possession.

Space taking activities need agreements. Children will not adapt if forced to share special toys or possessions, such as a computer, but they may enjoy showing off their skills by teaching a sibling or be willing to do a swop. Is there money for a cherished activity, martial arts or dance classes now that the finances are shared? If not, the new family will not be seen as a good move. So a subtle balance has to be made between two sets of customs which do not always fit neatly together. It was years later that the cat and guinea-pig story came up, as family history does. Then the young woman could tell her mother how she had felt as a child. All relationships are being constantly remade as everyone gets older and, with goodwill, sensitive subjects can be aired.

Adults attracted to each other usually have enough in common to make comfortable bonds and shared understandings which in turn lead the way to joint decisions. The children do not automatically have that. Neither do they have any reason to adapt customs to a new adult's attitude on how much pocket money or what time to go to bed or where they are allowed to hang out. In the end it is because the adults have got together that these can be a source of conflict and usually it is the adults who have the final say, preferably in consultation.

Pat and Andy have 'family meetings' where pocket money is set and jobs agreed. Martyn and Annette, with eight children, use the Quaker non confrontational approach which Martyn describes as, 'Non dogmatic. I believe in being prepared to compromise, the important thing is not to compel them.' Both believe that the experience of stepfamily life will, at the very least, give their eight children 'a tolerance of differing attitudes' Having so many children emphasizes the impossibility of imposing love or tolerance.

Private Space

Older children and young people often stake out their room or their shared space with a prominently displayed sign. This usually includes 'knock before you enter'. It is a good way for the ones who did not choose the stepfamily to make their wishes known and have some effect. They want privacy too. Adults take it for granted they deserve some peace and quiet and time in their own bedroom.

> *Stella liked making a display of precious things next to her bed in the room she shared with her sister. Her father and stepmother and stepsister all felt free to go into Stella's room anytime they were looking for something or wanted to speak to her or her sister. She did not like them touching her things or even looking at what she chose to put on her little shelf.* 'I saw she kept her mother's letters there in a little bundle and she had found a photo from where I have lots of old photos and put it in a frame. She was furious when I mentioned it. I had just never thought, but obviously she wanted it to be private,' *said her father feeling thoroughly insensitive and a touch put out that there were things going on inside his daughter she wanted to keep to herself.*

Jack may have the only private room to himself but there are penalties. Since Andy and Pat sleep in the living room their clothes are kept in a cupboard in Jack's room. Hence his insistence on them knocking first. Otherwise it is not really his room after all.

A Baby

Another reason for creating a boundary is when there is a new member of the stepfamily, the baby who has two parents in one home, the one whom others may have mixed feelings about. I still feel waves of guilt at the times our two-year-old went into his sister's extremely fascinating room and broke something precious. I was just too busy to make absolutely sure that he could not open the door. My attempt at fixing a bathroom-type bolt was good but not good enough. It is easy to fix things so you can say, I tried, but it is more of an effort to make respectful agreements and physical boundaries effective.

More often than not a baby who is half-brother or half-sister is welcomed and loved by the other children. But not necessarily at first. How do you tell them? Pat went home in trepidation and said to Jack, 'Do you want the good news first or the other? The good news is I can buy you Nintendo and the other is I'm pregnant.' Jack shut himself in the toilet for a long time. Many months later, however, he was thrilled and proud to relate that every card shop in the neighbourhood had sold out of baby girl congratulation cards.

Annette knew she wanted another child when she and Martyn got together. She had three with her first husband and Martyn had four so it was no casual agreement, even so, 'He came along earlier than planned.' Annette told her children but Martyn wanted to make sure his first wife heard this important information from him. The result was that his children heard from her children. It sounds a bit like the game of consequences.

This is one event that is best announced jointly. Alison and Ronnie sat down with his daughter and told her they would be having a baby who would be a sister or brother for her. After that they told other members of the family. A baby raises sensitivities for children not living with the parent and brings back memories for ex-partners and grandparents. Alison believes the baby helped her stepdaughter feel secure in the new family.

When I visited Martyn and Annette on a winter Sunday only the baby, now four-years-old, was at home with his parents. His train set covered the sitting-room floor with just the dog to get in the way of his game. This weekend is 'theirs', parents and child, as is every other one.

A Stepfamily Baby

- Make a joint announcement
- Tell the children first
- Be alert to insecurities about being loved
- Tell children what changes this will mean space, attention, activities,
- Accept children may not be pleased at first

The following weekend Martyn will spend with his children based at his house, which he has not been able to sell. The two parts of the family will visit and see each other as they feel like it. This stepfamily has been through several variations on the theme of stepfamily living and is still evolving to cope with children growing up and a depressed housing market. All families are constantly changing. As Martyn puts it, 'I want to provide somewhere my children feel at home and don't grow away because my life now seems separate from them.'

Chapter 5
Visiting Children – When is a child a stepchild?

'Was he married before?'

'Was he married? Taking over Buffy was like taking over a house full of sitting tenants.'

'Who was he married to?'

'A ghastly, neurotic woman called Jacquetta. They had two delinquent sons who used to come round every weekend and wreck the place. I had to be nice to them of course. Wicked stepmother and all that.'

The Ex-Wives by Deborah Moggach

WHEN IS A CHILD A STEPCHILD?

Brilliantly captured and extremely funny. And true, of course. Not easy though, to be so spot on when everything's more or less fine. Friendly youth do exist too and they may appear unexpectedly out of the black clad silent teens. Either sort is normal.

You may have children in the home plus visiting stepchildren or you may be a couple with a child joining you for weekends and holidays. The child's age will be the main determining factor in how closely the partner becomes involved in the detail of the child's life. And how you, as step-parent, feel about their other parent (that is the one whom the children live with) affects how you get on with the children too. You may be a big compensator or see them as an enemy, a small reproduction of your version of the 'ghastly, neurotic woman'. Sheila felt guilty every time the children came to stay because it reminded her that she was what used to be called the 'co-respondent' during the divorce proceeding as she had an affair and fell in love at the office Christmas party. Guilt is still a human emotion that trails depression and anger in its wake.

Sometimes the parent's worry of getting everything right when the child arrives for this all important contact means he turns to his partner for help. He needs her there to confirm that everything is fine and that it is a proper, happy family or to alleviate adult terror at having to cope alone with an expectant or confused child.

You don't have to do everything together. But when you know how important the visits are to your partner it is tough to see a look of consternation or incomprehension on his face as you leave parent and children to each other. What you can do, instead of holding on tightly to your small bit of independent life or plunging in with total foolhardiness, is to talk about visits beforehand which will give you a chance to say what you want and what you will feel comfortable with.

The other side of this is feeling excluded when the parent, she or he, does want to spend time alone with the children and lets them do things you would not do in your home or spend money you regard as joint income. There isn't a fixed answer, but there is a real pay off to trust. And it doesn't become an arguing issue then if you leave it to the parent. The visit shows instead you are supportive and can step back without reacting from hidden jealousies.

Most part-time steps feel obliged to show their interest and commitment by being there and make an effort to join in and being nice to them while they wreck, if not your home, wreck your nerves, wreck your relationship, as you see the love of your life behaving in a strange, unrecognizable manner. Is he too impatient with them? Or too lenient? Or does he give them all his attention and you none? Does all sharing go out the window and you start to feel like a servant servicing an invader?

When the children arrive they can bring a natural injection of energy and make a renewed, expanded family. Or your life may undergo a brief but radical change. Just take the opportunity to do something as an individual and leave the parent some time with their child, one to one. It depends on the age of the child, as well as your inclinations, on how much you want to be involved. The younger the child the more inclination to expect them to fit in with you. Little children cannot be avoided and neither do they ignore the other people who live with their parent. If they take to you they will want to sit on your lap and ask endless questions, whatever they think of you and they will untidy your home and investigate your private belongings.

Step Mother?

'She wanted to hold my hand and be cuddled and it drove me crazy. I liked it a bit but it became an endless demand. In the end I insisted Mike do something with her that gave me a break, like bathing her or anything where we weren't in the same room all the time. I even willingly did all the meals so I could be alone in the kitchen. I felt guilty and critical, imagining that her mother must be very cold to her and yet I was pushing her away.' *Brenda felt reluctant to talk about her feelings to Mike thinking he would feel very unsupported when he was trying to be a dad but eventually she did and just talking about her feelings helped.* 'I tried not to say his daughter was a pain but said I wasn't used to a child and didn't know how to handle the constant needs. That did help. I can laugh now seeing Mike trying to be the sensitive man for two complicated females. She was only three.'

It is not unusual for a visiting small child to expect all the adults in what he perceives as the extended family to want to mother him or to respond to him in a friendly, caring sort of way. A small child who is used to being the centre of attention will expect all big people to attend to him. It's the egocentric time of life.

Partner Not Parent?

Susie is a young stepmother to Jude or maybe more like an elder sister. She's twenty two and he is ten. Jude comes to visit from a small town in Scotland where he lives with his mother, his stepfather of several years and his two younger half-sisters.

His home there is a well established group of adults and children. The contact between Jude and his father, Pete, has been erratic. Since Susie and Pete have been living together this has changed and now he wants to see more of his son and play a bigger part in his life. Maybe this is partly maturity, Pete is now thirty six, and some of it is surely the effects of love and relative stability. So what does Susie say? 'I don't see myself as a stepmother, that's definite. I am his dad's girl friend, serious girl friend, we're going to get married so obviously Jude and I are going to get to know each other well. When he's here I treat him like any child visitor, make him feel at home and make sure he's got things to do or play with because he is after all completely dependent on us. He doesn't know any one else and we live in a flat in quite a run down area of Bristol. He's a bit shy of both of us but I would say Jude and I get on fine.'

'It's seeing Pete's disappointment if Jude isn't that affectionate and listening to what Jude's visits bring up from the past, that's the hard part. I remember my mother being angry towards my father because he didn't keep to arrangements or maintenance. How I deal with this is I've decided it's not my problem or my business, outside of listening to Pete because I care about how he feels. As far as I can I support Pete as a parent.'

I can imagine that this young woman would make any child welcome in her home. She sounds clear about not being drawn into Pete's responsibilities, seeing her role as supporting Pete's newly awakened fatherhood, and that sets a firm base for the future in which her own links with Jude can develop at a natural pace.

'What I refuse to get involved with is things to do with money and I know Pete needs to complain about Jude's mother but I don't join in. I sympathize with how he feels, naturally, but Pete knows I'm not interested in taking sides. I mean I don't even know her.'

All children have a life and interests which they are most likely to be leaving behind in order to visit a parent. Some of course live in the same area and their social life can carry on. Whichever it is, there is almost always a gain and a loss. There is that classic picture of the Sunday father who does things with his child that he would never have done before the divorce – the park, the swimming pool, skating, endless outings to avoid a home which is not geared for children, or welcoming. Whatever age no-one can turn themselves into the perfect theme park home for a visiting stepchild but a space, however much it resembles indoor camping, can be as homely and be enjoyed as any room.

Occasionally I hear determined statements about how the stepchild has to 'fit in'. He might do just that if a place, physical or emotional is clearly defined and attractive, which he is encouraged to make his own.

There will be times when you can act as the joint adult of the house, making the children feel at home, drawing them into what you enjoy. When we're having fun the lines of my parent, my spouse tend to disappear in an at home feeling.

Some stepmothers appear to take a great delight in being able to say, 'they arrive with no change of clothes or no clean clothes' or something that is frankly critical on a very basic level. It is a tempting way to make oneself feel good and necessary. Stepfathers do the same on a discipline level. 'They don't know how to behave,' another way of 'licking into shape.'

When we're unsure of our position, resenting the fact that our home is also our stepchild's home, it is easy to slip into a traditional, authoritarian attitude and our tolerance of human imperfection fades rapidly. These critical comments also give a role and a purpose to the adult and child relationship. Achieving a balance in positive and helpful comment will be part of that bonding; when comment is negative or bossy neither party will enjoy the visit.

The older child will have a lifestyle and tastes that are already set. These may be mysterious to you or may even evoke powerful memories of excitement – all those late night parties and deep conversations – or danger, drugs, coming home late, and unreasonable requests to be collected from far-flung events.

Be grateful it isn't full time. Don't be afraid to ask the other parent how he or she copes in these situations. The parent who has main care and residency will have gone through it all and hopefully will say what is acceptable and why and what isn't. You can do things differently but gain some free wisdom from the conversation. Don't be too proud to ask for advice.

A Step Back

'I've spent so much of my life avoiding family life and I've married a man with four children after living alone for twelve years.' *Ruth has to laugh at herself which is just as well since her husband's stormy relationship with his ex-wife carries over and causes divided loyalties for the children. The visits are loaded with mixed feelings. They don't all visit at the same time, even so Ruth can feel quite sidelined by the powerful and long-established bonds between father and children.*

She is absolutely determined to take it slowly and be true to herself. She describes herself as 'actually quite shy' *often preferring to retire to her room and to get on with her own things.* 'We have supper and tell jokes and watch TV but we don't ever talk about us. They don't know how to be with me anymore than I know how to be with them. And the girls are young women, 17 and 15, and will be separating from him soon enough and I come along and marry their Dad.' *At 46, Ruth wants neither to be a parent nor a step-parent and accepts that a real solid relationship will take time. For her it is essential to know when to be alert to signals of appreciation and when the message is leave it alone.*

After two and a half years of living together and after four months of marriage she now gets covert signs of approval by the children: flowers for· her birthday left on the table, and a message on the answerphone. On her part Ruth is putting out a few signals herself. 'Ben is here – he's 14 – and we've just been to play bowls. Six months ago I wouldn't have gone, I feel more able and more willing to join in and I suspect I have to learn more about recognizing the signals, mine and their's and what we all feel comfortable with.'

Parent's Partner – The Girlfriend

Before the children arrive consider and discuss with your partner whether you want to take equal responsibility for the children when they visit. Welcoming is one thing and taking on the parent role is quite a huge step on.

> *Paulette had children from a previous marriage and a child with Steven. She continued to be very much the household mum when his son and daughter came to visit in the holidays and is inextricably bound up with his children. One of Steven's children got on her nerves.*
>
> 'Whatever Miles does it would be the wrong thing, he'll break something or lose it and I can't even stand the sound of his voice. Steven is very protective of him. But both Steven's children like being with mine, so that helps me cope with feeling so tense. I try not to show the children. Fiona is real friends with my daughter. They usually visit separately and if Steve spends time with Miles it is painful for me because Steve doesn't want to be close with my children.'
>
> *The family lived in Wales and Paulette takes her children off to the beach for a Sunday walk so that Steven and his child can have some time together free of any stray resentment. There is not much room in the tiny house so the two boys camp in the tiny garden. They love it.*

Considering the conflicting emotions in this stepfamily their strategies were:

- accept that it worked if one child came at a time
- that Steven needed exclusive time with his children
- that Paulette made decisions on how the home functioned,
  on household jobs, bedtimes and noise levels.

Despite taking on the unattractive aspects of the parental role Paulette expresses her satisfaction at having this control. 'I'm happy with that as what happens isn't questioned. After so many years and some hard moments we're feeling more relaxed now.'

Parent's Partner – The Boyfriend

Is it any easier for a man when children visit their mother? Many of the same considerations apply after all; questions of space, their space to feel at home, being made welcome by the parent's partner, getting involved or not and knowing when to leave parent and child alone.

Jeff has been living with Lottie on and off for three years. Her sons are 14 and 16 and argue fiercely. Jeff has daughters, a few years older, who tell him frequently what a wickedly wonderful dad he is and how much they love him. He admits part of that is compensation as they do not live with him even so he is appalled at the two boys as they head into full-blown adolescence. 'Once or twice I did get involved and Lottie really didn't like it. What provoked me to act, sometimes against my better judgement, was them treating her badly. I don't mind them behaving badly with each other. So I weighed in and told them to show her a bit of respect.'

I could practically see the steam rising from Jeff. It is hard to watch someone you love getting trampled on by careless youth and strange when that person is normally a strong woman and, compared to his experience of his visiting teenage daughters, this was tough. He decided that the best way to cope was to help Lottie by talking things through with her so she felt less overwhelmed. 'I think I help best by giving her another point of view, another perspective, without being judgemental. That's important when she sees them so little, she doesn't want me telling her how awful they are because she loves them.'

The normal rivalry of brothers close in age is heightened by arriving from the country to spend a weekend in a small city flat living at close quarters with each other. Lottie makes a big effort and plans all sorts of activities so they that can't fail to have a great time. On top of that here is this sensible guy they have to make a relationship with but they haven't come to see him, though good on computers and can be handy with homework.

Another useful role Jeff plays is being there for Lottie when she crumples after a phone call from her ex-partner and to fix things like the birthday bike jumped on by the other brother in a fit of rage.

If all this sounds too much like stereotypes then Jeff feels that it is revealing to be allowed into a different side of Lottie's character. Women have come into their own in the last decade as managers and professionals and for Lottie, used to planning schedules and organizing staff or other similar responsibilities, it has become a bit shameful to show weakness or hurt and doubt in one's ability in the more personal areas. Even so Jeff is aware that it doesn't mean going in as the strong man and staying there.

The Message
These partners of parents say:

- let the parents do things their way
- remember their time together is short
- support your partner, don't criticize
- don't judge his or her child
- as for the direct relationship with visiting child – let it grow slowly.

Avoid Trouble
The children are your partner's responsibility but rather than be at the mercy of their emotions, set up situations for good company.

- little ones –   set up activities they enjoy.
  making biscuits, painting models,
  swimming, skating
  a happy child is a trouble free one
- adolescents –   check partner's share of action care e.g.
  haircuts, clothes buying can be fun and
  good bonding

63

> bowling, football, bike mending
> let them bring a friend – it's home,
> remember?

- Adults' plan in advance
  > ask your kids' advice on making
  > partner's children feel welcome
  > make boundaries clear to the children
  > don't be all together all the time

Choose Your Style

- Homely weekend
- Devoted to children
- Parent responsible or couple?
- Keep them simple
- Decide what is/isn't flexible
- Special outings
- Mix of your time – their time
- Decide your dos and don'ts
- Explain – short and sweet
- Row when they've gone

Chapter 6
Step-parent and birth parent
ADULTS GETTING ON

IT IS POSSIBLE for the step-parent to have a reasonable working relationship with the birth parent. The birth parent is always going to be one of the two most important and irreplaceable people in the lives of the children. The step-parent is not a substitute for the birth parent but a new and different person in the family.

Confidence

Just because there has been a relationship to the same partner does not mean birth parent and step-parent feel any affinity towards each other. The connection is through the children. You may or may not have other interests and tastes in common. You may like each other or distrust each other. Nevertheless, a reasonable relationship is possible and, however little you see of each other the relationship still exists, humming through the airwaves, unseen and perhaps unspoken but definitely felt.

The more self-confident you are in yourself and in your position as the chosen partner and friendly step-parent, the less you will be at the mercy of any leftover discord between the parents. Don't forget that even if you chose your partner and only later realized what being part of a stepfamily involved, you still made that choice and picked out that partner from the whole world. Hopefully there are still many good aspects of that choice.

Naturally it helps if the other parent is happy. It is much easier to co-operate if the birth parent is feeling good about a new life. Does it feel as though there is an onlooker on the margins of your marriage, a 'hungry ghost', as the Chinese say, who never moved on and who is constantly hankering for the lost relationship?

Money

You may be paying maintenance or receiving it or both if the two adults in the stepfamily have children, some resident and some visiting. Money, the lack of it, the unreliability of its arrival, and many other details of this essential item, is a good guideline for measuring your feelings towards your counterpart. Mark just doesn't have anything to do with the father of his stepchildren. 'If he rings and I pick up the phone I just pass it over. The very low amount of money he pays towards the children means a certain amount of tension. I have come to accept that's how it is and decided to let it go.'

It would be easy to focus on this as a useful grudge when the stepfather supports several stepchildren, and his own first family. If you accept it's impossible to get on then leaving things alone is probably the best you can do. Don't join your partner in criticizing and running down that 'ghost' of the former relationship, however tempting. Separate your relationship with the birth parent from that of your partner's. A trouble shared can be a trouble doubled. Listen but leave it alone. Your sensitivity and, frankly, good manners could make all the difference to someone who feels usurped. It may be that the 'hungry ghost' has good reasons for feeling deprived, especially where money is concerned. It is better to have things out in the open about maintenance and best to accept the imperfections. Your partner may not be as rational and honest with himself or herself about the divorce or separation arrangements as it may appear. Don't let your partner's anger, guilt and responsibility cloud your attitude toward the other parent.

A couple who each came to their second marriage with two children had comfortable and flexible arrangements over the children and, since the husband was the main but not sole provider for the stepfamily, she wisely stayed out of his wish to help his first wife sort out her money muddles. The stepfamily had a good income. The first wife had spent her portion from the sale of the original family home and Pam, the second wife, was critical of the first wife's attitude to finance but is willing to accept that this is part of a relationship that doesn't always come to a neat end. 'Personally, I think she's been a bit silly to spend the money without doing something sensible with it but . . .'

It is an unhappy fact that women, for many centuries chattels and dependents, are only now gaining the confidence to handle and make money work for them. Some control over income brings a feeling of independence. Pam had a job and her salary went into the joint household account, but it nevertheless gave her a sense of independence and confidence which lessened any feeling of competition towards the first wife. The two women were not active friends but they did have a sensible contact which included knowing when to leave things alone. Pam appreciated her husband's good qualities which included – with slight reservations – caring about his first wife's finances and for the mother of his children.

However, money is not the only link between parent and step-parent. When the stepmother in particular has everyday care for another woman's children the pressures to become either good friends or steely-eyed rivals are greater.

Co-operating

Jean had two children and three stepchildren who lived with her and their father. Jean's stepchildren went to stay with their mother for part of the holidays but the main home was with Jean and David. Occasionally their mother Cassie, who lived at the opposite end of the country, came to stay for a few days. Both the women wanted to make these visits relaxed and friendly.

'One of the children I found hard work, somehow whatever I did it was like pouring love into a sieve, she was such a whiny little thing. Once when Cassie was here she stayed home with a "tummy ache" and we were sitting over a coffee in the kitchen, chatting and she had her arm round her mother and looked so contented, so shiningly happy. It had a big effect on me and I stopped trying so hard – probably without realizing it – to be a replacement, and from that moment I never forgot that Cassie was her mother. And that I could just be me. It was as if her being miserable must be a reflection on me. I stopped feeling I was totally responsible for making everyone happy and being annoyed when they weren't.'

That was a sixties story when it was assumed that people and their relationships were at their best when spontaneous and informal. And, in spite of the bad press, there were some good aspects of this. Jean explained that it would not have occurred to her to refuse to have the children's mother to stay even though in her imagination Cassie was the first and, therefore, the foremost woman in her man's life. Cassie was clever, blonde and a karate black belt. Jean was dark and cooked the meals, 'I did feel like that poster about a relationship beginning by sinking into his arms and ending with your arms in his sink. I couldn't help comparing myself involuntarily because she was always spoken about as if she was so extraordinary that I felt I was just a sensible replacement. But in practice Cassie and I just liked each other, and in some ways it was David who got a bit left out.'

Formal Or Informal?

So what about the other side, Jean's children and the absent father? Well, he too came to visit. In cool macho sixties style he just called in to see how his progeny were, accompanied by his current girl friend. That easy going style was fine for the adults in this family. Seeing another man around his children who enjoyed family life, who was practical and did things with the children, gave this absent father a bit of a shock. He surprised Jean and the children by actually visiting them rather than the other way round. These children saw that their parents accepted each other, were welcomed, talked, ate and drank together, at the same time the stepfamily was the focus of their lives. However, the informal option doesn't work for everyone. Children need to know what arrangements have been agreed and to feel that they are part of it. Jean's children would have liked a more reliable, predictable contact with their father and David's children did have divided loyalties between him as the custodial father and their absent mother. 'We weren't consulted' is a common cry children make in retrospect.

Nowadays, in the nineties adults are more aware that children's wishes need to be considered. There is more talk with everyone taking part in decision making. The key words now are communication and rights rather than peace and love.

When a Parent Visits

A parent coming to stay can be hard for the visited stepfamily because, whether it is for an afternoon or a few days, there is rarely enough room to escape each other for a few moments. The stepfamily is seen dealing with the practical things like who's doing the washing up and the obvious side of the new relationship is on show but not the subtleties.

Life can continue with most of the usual arrangements but some time needs to be set aside to make the visitor feel welcome and provide the opportunity to say clearly that one to one time between parent and child is fine too.

Start with an open conversation and show that you expect to be flexible. 'What would you like to do while you're here?' Jean and David lived in the country so, when the pressure was on, someone could go outside or for a walk with several children. The garden took away some of the pressures of being too close, crammed into the sitting room. Visiting by either absent parent is easier in good weather or at least in the spring and summer. In towns or cities there are plenty of local events.

Children want their separated parents to get on well and more than once I have heard a parent say, 'He loves it when we are all here on his birthday.' Or 'She enjoys it so much when her dad comes round and we all do something together.' Sounds wonderful. That is the parent talking about the child's response to having

69

parents and step-parents together. Fortunately, some step-parents and ex-partners have a willingness to see what is possible. If that is not possible plan in advance how much time you can cope with spending together. When Cassie, who lived on the other side of the country, came for a few days she went to a parents' evening with her ex-husband. She also had time alone with her children while Jean and partner went out for the evening.

The closest co-operation I've seen in action between parent and step-parent is in a village where the first wife and two children moved into a house opposite her ex-husband, his new partner and their child. Liz made me coffee and said 'No milk! I'll just run over and see if Caroline's got some.' I was impressed. Later the older children arrived back from a Christian summer festival and ran over to see their father. In such close proximity the mother and stepmother had to co-operate but it was more than that. It's tempting to believe this is real Christianity in action. There was no doubt, Liz confirmed, that the children, 11 and 13, positively wanted the adults to be close in body and spirit.

'I would really enjoy going away one Christmas but they love us all being together and I couldn't deny them that.' It certainly eases friendly terms between stepmother and mother living in the same village when there is a useful agreement over babysitting and, for Caroline and Liz, this extended to after-school care. 'Our separation was friendly, Charlie is great but impossible to live with. I'd rather we all got on well than argue over financial support so I don't rely on his unreliable work as a builder. Much better for the children if he can keep his home together and this way I can get back from college and know they're fine.'

Some lives seem to be inextricably linked. Bill met his second wife, Sarah, while helping his ex-wife, Isabelle, to move into her new home, the home where Sarah grew up.

Boundaries

Sarah has two young children and a visiting stepson. She had to put a distance between her and Bill's first wife because as she says, 'I feel she would like to be much more involved but I hate it. I just can't handle it. It's like she's still married and

70

needs Bill to do things for her all the time which he is willing to do because they have a child. So I have decided what is my territory and my space and I need to protect that.'

'Before I made this decision I felt put down, felt that someone was interfering all the time although I know it wasn't meant like that. I need my marriage to have some privacy from Isabelle.' *Sarah is not noticeably younger than Isabelle now but, ten years ago, when Sarah married Bill, the six years' difference enhanced her feelings of vulnerability towards the more dominant and older personality.*

Attitudes And Understanding

Adults may choose their partner but not their partner's ex-spouse. They may be aware of all kinds of intimate gossip and criticism about each other even before they meet so it is impossible to behave and respond in the usual social manner. They do not begin at the beginning and, gradually, get to know each other rather it is more the other way round, from close up to realistic perspective.

The absent parent can be seen as simply absent, the one who caused all the problems, screwed up the children, who does what she or he wants, the rival, or the more powerful. Generally speaking, the more contact there is between all the parents the greater the understanding and the fewer the illusions.

Kim, stepmother to two children, talked of coming to accept and know the mother. 'Carol, their mother, had this idea we lived in the lap of luxury and after we met – in family therapy so you can guess the stress – there were no more myths, not a dragon on the end of the phone, just a real person. I can't say family therapy solved much but resentments were voiced and it was good for her and me to hear each other and we did get on much better.'

'Until then there was always an awkwardness about her existence. I found it difficult that the ex-wife was always present in some way, either she was phoning or Don had to consider her. He felt he had broken the ultimate trust when they broke up. And I suppose what I felt was a sort of

71

jealousy of their past. At the same time I knew from Don talking about her that she was my kind of person.'

Attitudes
When was the last time you mentioned the other parent?
Was it positive or negative?
Outwardly – are you frank? tactful?
Inwardly – self-righteous? healthily critical? Or secretly hostile?
How is it when you answer the phone and it is her or him?
Brief, brief and polite, brief and friendly?
What is good about your relationship with the other parent?
What isn't so good?
What would you like to change? What could you do to improve that?
Choose one single, small act you could take immediately. Do it. How did it feel? What is the reward?

Advantages
If there are advantages associated with the birth parent then the atmosphere can be cordial and appreciative. Everyone benefits. What could these advantages be? Make your list. However difficult your situation, there must be one advantage. Can that be cultivated? When you've noted the advantages for you, then look at the list at the end of this chapter where you will find practical ways of making the most of this relationship.

Co-operation over access, visits and holidays are easier and more flexible when the parents and step-parents live within easy travelling distance. This may already be a fixed item but it does make a difference if one set of parents moves further away and does not think to consider or talk over what this means with regard to visits and right of access. A very common comment by children is that they were not asked if that is what they wanted or even told in advance, but it just happened. The same is true of ex-partners. They are affected.

Eileen's stepchildren came to visit most weekends and then their mother moved home which involved hours of travel. There was neither consultation, nor any warning. Eileen, the step-mother and the birth mother do not talk to each other or have any outward contact. However, Eileen felt that moving the children so far away was a powerful message. There was huge resentment towards the woman whose late decisions or unpredictable behaviour affected all the family.

'She is a very competent lady,' *affirms Eileen politely, attempting to be strictly truthful.* 'At the start I tried desperately hard to be friends as I am friends with my ex-husband and his wife, so that seems normal. We did have a nodding relationship when we lived nearer but I ended up accepting she is very bolshie, very arrogant. Even so I never criticize her in front of the children and, since I'm older, I don't compete as a mother.'

'We are both working and she's not, therefore we spend huge amounts on travel every year. We do a 500 mile round trip every six weeks. She's living on the state and we pay, yet we have no say. If Roy sees his children it costs us a lot of money. And because Roy's wife went bankrupt this muddies the relations even more. His attitude is it's all for the benefit of the children.'

In common with other second partners, Eileen is deeply affected by what she sees and experiences as angry, damaging and almost vengeful behaviour towards her partner by his wife. She can't stay out of it because it does also affect her life and this is where the dreaded initials appear – C. S. A. – Child Support Agency. Gradually the couple have negotiated some agreement with the C. S. A. on the value of their contributions in kind, as for example college books.

If you move house or take a holiday or even if there are changes in your employment remember to let the other parent know before not after as these will affect the access arrangements. The children's other parent does not want to be part of your family or be an afterthought, but may well want to be another active parent. The children will notice. If they see that you both bear their other parent in mind it prevents crises of divided loyalty and gives them confidence that mum or dad won't be left out. We may feel that we have covered every angle but we do need to realize the repercussion and consequences that our a new arrangements might have.

When To Let Go

As the children get older they do feel as if they need more say when the parent and stepfamily live reasonably near. It is usually at this point when older children go directly to their birth parents that a step-parent may need to reconsider his role. It may be time to let go a bit now. Evelyn found herself feeling quite hurt after so many years of being stepmum when her stepsons spent more and more time at their mother's place. 'It was as if they felt it wasn't particularly any business of mine. I admit I did feel unimportant really after such a long time.'

If you know the parent as a person, however slightly, a low-key phone call won't seem odd. You won't suddenly need introducing. You or your partner do need to know where teenagers are. The other parent may have taken it for granted that you both know they're with her or him.

It can be peculiar to realize that after all those years when you have had to carefully weigh the feelings of other people that now the parent and children make their own arrangements and it is not altogether your business any more. You fell in love with your partner not the children and now you've got the chance to concentrate on just the two of you.

Clear Arrangements

Like any family, the members need to remember to let each other know where they are and when they'll be back. That feeling of being treated casually is at the bottom of many rows or simmering resentment. You do need to know if the children are at the other parent's home, and the converse is just as important. Parents are not automatically at home either and you need to say when you'll be back. Teenagers can feel they've fallen through a gap between two families and the other parent will feel casually treated too.

The Right Decision For You

However, you may be part of an extended family that isn't willing to co-operate or able to be friendly. You may breathe a sigh of relief when the other parent is so far away that clear arrangements have to be made.

- decide who pays travel costs and when
- decide who delivers and collects
- decide what's safe for the child
- compare cost of travel to cost of children at home
- quiet time without stepchildren is worth quite a bit

It is a burden when three children go to Cornwall by train three times a year and the other parent pleads poverty and you have to pay the costs. Weigh up the cost of sending them and compare that with the money you would have spent if they had stayed at home. There could be more advantages for you to have time without the stepchildren, with your beloved, with your own children. When your stepchildren are relaxed, happy and confident after seeing their parent you benefit also. Being morally superior is a popular option but so often it ends up becoming a method of cutting off one's nose to spite one's face.

If the other parent's reasonable demands are met then he (or she) will know that you are not necessarily out to supplant him or put him down in subtle ways in the eyes of his own children. Children do worry about the adults in their lives. It is reassuring when those adults seem to be coping sensibly.

In Paul's situation it was hard for him and his wife to see the children stay with their father who had been in prison and whom he described as having a problem with drink and violence. They believed the children wanted to go sometimes but felt they were also afraid to say no if they didn't want to visit. 'They see him most Sundays and we try to have a balance of the children deciding and us as adults knowing what's best. In general terms he's from a more traditional background and I'm more of a new man. The children are looking at the adults all the time, I don't know whether they compare us but at least they see that he isn't excluded.'

When, as in Tom's stepfamily, wife and the birth father fight over just about everything, how much is it the step-parent's affair? As he said, 'Really I wonder how they ever got together. It is such a lethal mixture. I'm sure I could get on fine with him and our marriage isn't like that, fighting, but now I've worked it out, I just stay out of it. I can see he would even like to just chat or exchange a few words but I can stay away from their unresolved things best if I am strictly polite.' Tom does his bit by taking and collecting the children so the father does not come to the stepfamily home. He believes his uncompromising detachment is understood by the father and underlines his loyalty to his wife and also his own independence. 'She knows I won't get involved with her old wounds, otherwise I feel as if I married them both and joined in their past.' Power is a key word. If there are disagreements, even physical fights, each see the other as holding the power. The step-parent can be drawn into these struggles to establish a new post-divorce relationship related to residence, visits, holidays and who buys the biggest presents.

- Is it a feeling, a point of view or does power actually reside in actions?
- Have you like Tom and Kim felt caught in the middle of unresolved past business between her and him?
- What makes you feel powerless?
- Have you taken some action or decision, small or big that altered the way you saw your place in the power scale of the stepfamily?

You may be pleased with the way you and the other parent handle the fact that you both belong to the same extended family. You may remain unaffected by your partner's past. You may be less of a step-parent and more of a friend, even a role model or mentor; or just mum's husband or dad's wife who leaves bringing up the children to the birth parents. It is easier to do this in some families where the step-parent is perhaps not much older than the older children. Or there can be the feeling of being left out as a young person in between the children and the grown-ups who are ex-partners. Most of us need the security that comes from a balance of protectiveness and generosity in our dealings with our stepchild's parent. When we do feel able to make a small gesture, a warmer tone of voice when answering the phone or active friendliness it brings rewards. In the end our boundaries are made by us, not by someone else.

Advantages Checklist

- A friend and ally
- Fair arrangements over holidays
- Stepchildren see you as friends
- Stepchildren trust you
- Stepchildren can't play one against another
- Your partner can't play one against another (can be a subtle one this)
- Less competition, e.g. the other earns more, looks younger, is cleverer
- You know each other's faults
- Time off from children – time with partner – time for your life
- Space for romance – undisturbed and unhurried sex
- Confidence in your role

Chapter 7
Home Rules

Now they are two strapping young men . . . whom I still
have to hassle about taking out the garbage and making
their beds, but we are good friends and can laugh about the
fearsome pitched battles of the past . . . I lost every battle
with them but, miraculously, I think I am winning the war.

from *Paula* by Isabel Allende

DISORDER AND HARMONY

The writer above is talking of her stepsons, one of whom was the
stepson of her husband from a previous marriage and so doubly a step.
It is a great image, these strong and amiable young men. They still need
a push but they're willing now in contrast to the tough early days and
even more so, the nights. The ten-year-old banging on the bedroom
door in a jealous rage and another, older stepson heavily into drugs are
potential situations that any parent and step-parent may face.

Accepted wisdom has it that the parent is responsible for discipline. And that this works is explained by one teenage girl: 'If dad tells
me to do something he means it. I'm not told to do things all the time
at dad and Sandra's, although I do babysit, and I like the feeling of not
being pressurized, Sandra doesn't expect me to be always helping.
Sometimes I disagree with her and he has to sort it out.'

So what happens when the parent is away and the step-parent is
left in charge? That's the moment when everyone can behave out
of character. The good girl, her stepmother's friend and ally says
no when you ask her to tidy her room. She wants to do something
else and a most unexpected battle begins as she refuses to stay in
her allotted role. Recognize the scene?

Or this one perhaps? 'Tony was out and Caroline and Alex were
arguing and it turned into a fight. I didn't know what to do. Of
course I went over the top and it ended up with me throwing them

out of the house. They went round to their mum's which was a bit embarrassing, but I did make a point of leaving the mess so Tony could see what had happened.' No parent wants to believe that the children are impossible, what used to be called 'badly brought up'. It reflects on them as parents. Most of all parents want their partners to think well of them as parents, capable of setting routine rules and coping with explosive situations. The way in which we respond to our children within the stepfamily is a delicate area. Each adult needs to feel the support and approval of the other, and that may not always be there because few of us have exactly the same approaches to bringing up children.

Finding The Right Approach

We may not automatically approve of our partner's attitude towards discipline and may be horrified by what seems unnecessary strictness or archaic ways of influencing behaviour. I have been shocked and disturbed by a stepmother washing out a four-year-old child's mouth with soap because he swore. She was obviously shocked and disturbed by a small child swearing. It is essential to talk about what level of discipline you both feel comfortable with at a time when you are both relaxed. It can be frightening to discover at a time of tension or in the middle of a family row that an unbridgeable chasm is opening up between you. Talk about what you believe in doing yourself, such as loss of pocket money or a few fixed rules, like no swearing and no fighting, and what disturbs you in the other person's style of discipline. Total agreement on discipline is rare and some couples agree that each will take the approach that suits them best. Selma and Chris do not accept agreeing to differ but want to work out something that underlies the whole way they and their children live together.

'It's a parallel journey really,' explains Chris, 'we really listen to the children and look at our own feelings which come from the way we grew up.' The idea is that this listening allows the children to go right through angry or competitive feelings towards any other member of the family whether adult or child and, instead of the parent or step-parent sorting out an argument, Selma and Chris get them to listen to each other. All this doesn't just happen, it is not a spontaneous style of dealing with difficult feelings. Selma and Chris work on it together by reading the books by Adele Faber and Elaine Mazlish which describe the listening methods and the concepts behind this approach to children's behaviour.

These methods include listening without interruption, listening without reacting to the words and avoiding blame phrases such as 'don't annoy me or why do you always have to shout' but taking time to see what emotions are behind the rudeness, whininess or anger. Faber and Mazlish believe parents can defuse tensions and repeat clashes by saying, for example 'I know it's hard to share a room. Think for five minutes and tell me what will make easier.' Then listen again giving the child full attention. Other parenting exercises include not moving in to sort out children's problems for them but supporting their efforts and sticking to agreements such as no sweets before tea, homework before television. 'We read together in bed in the morning (they have a 3-month-old baby so before the other three children are up) and look at what we do and also how we were treated. We notice the patterns of what goes on and how we react. Agreeing to disagree is useless.' Selma says that with this discipline through listening it is all right for the children to '*show their ugly feelings*'. She did not react with hurt feelings or anger when her daughter said she hated the coming baby and it is true that the twelve-year-old loves her sister now she is here. This may not be a direct result of expressing the jealousy but simply of having a sister after two lively brothers, but who knows. This listening method sounds time consuming at first and self-conscious. Selma described it similar to learning a new language, exchanging the negative 'Why can't you . . . You never . . .' for the positive 'I know you can. . .'

If this sounds hard work do you have a chosen method or do you play it by ear? The latter can work fine but is liable to let you down in the really tricky moments. And how do you feel about your partner's approach to bad behaviour? Is it bearable to accept the odd outburst from a partner who is usually easygoing and tolerant? You may prefer this or the listening and exploring method toward discipline as above may suit you or you may feel comfortable with a partner who has very definite dos and don'ts. As one stepfather said, a little wearily, 'Then there's always a new situation to deal with as they get older.'

Expectations

Should the expectations from stepchildren be any different from those of any other children? Such as, reasonable politeness, doing homework, no hitting, no stealing. They are first and foremost children, who will be annoying sometimes, have irritating habits and incomprehensible tastes, behave badly, feel angry and have to deal with situations that upset them. All these experiences are common in the daily ebb and flow of emotion and reason.

As adults we have understanding friends we can complain to, expecting sympathy and constructive comments. Children whether stepchildren or not are not wild animals to be controlled and kept quiet. They respond, as we adults do, to simple requests and to people who are genuine and straightforward. It may sound like a cliché but aggression and other attention-seeking behaviour is a kind of sign language too. As well as dealing with any immediate clashes, give the children a chance to complain and talk about their view of the stepfamily. Jaw jaw is better than war war.

Discipline is different in a stepfamily because initially the child may not recognize the step-parent as equal to the parent. That can make the step-parent feel like a powerless outsider in the family home. Insistence on imposing rules often makes for more tension. Mark explains his approach which took into consideration the fact that his stepchildren came into his home.

'I eased myself into the discipline aspect gradually. The first year I was getting used to them and they were settling in what was my home. I knew it would be hard going for me sometimes as I was new to parenthood. We do try to show a united approach and, even if we don't completely agree with the way the other person is dealing with something, we support each other. In practice the older children 17 and 15 look to Jill and with the younger ones 12 and 9 I'm daddy and they accept what I say.'

Age does make a difference: the younger boys have known Mark, their stepfather for a large part of their childhood, five years is a steady length of time for them. He sees that what suits him and the younger boys would not suit the older children at all. Discipline is used in a discriminating manner.

81

Parents comment frequently that the husband or wife is over-critical of the stepchildren's behaviour and of their partner's parenting skills. The step-parent believes he or she knows better and is keen to say so, thus undermining the parent's confidence. In different ways this is true of both stepmothers and stepfathers and also appears to arise from good intentions: namely a desire to put things right, to make things better, to create harmony and to play an important role in the new household. But step-parents do not have to take on everything, and it is sensible to say, 'You know the child best and I'm going to leave big issues to you. If you're not there I'll do things my way.'

Seen As The Strict One

Paul has been married for two years and was involved with his wife for a year before that. He has a stepdaughter of twelve and a stepson of ten. He gets on fine with the boy but not with his stepdaughter.

'Being a parent is hard, being a step-parent is harder and the older the child the harder. I steamed in and said we're going to do things this way. But as they were nine and seven in lots of ways attitudes were already set. Now I'd say there's a need to accept children as they are and to realize that change is slow. Now I am ready to agree to disagree.'

That sounds realistic and reasoned, and yet a little sad as Paul's earlier optimism slipped away. He moved from seeing himself as someone who wanted to improve the quality of life for the family to accepting that there are going to be clashes with his stepdaughter. Paul has a son who visits but does not live with them so he had experience as well as ideas on discipline. Even so his new situation is a familiar one, namely, 'I'm seen as the strict one in the family and the children do play you off. I've been through feelings of being so undermined.'

He and his wife talked about how to share responsibility for children in the home and at first it was a bit of a no-win situation. If Paul took a back seat, his wife felt it was all being left to her, and, as the children got older, new versions of old situations arose. In addition to this was Paul's disappointment and hurt at his stepdaughter's resentment. Anyone who has been a step-parent knows the angry strength of the child whose life has changed. Yet, it was Paul who felt the powerless one.

Conflict Resolution

However, there are strategies which can help relieve these conflicts. Paul and Cathy agreed to be more supportive and positive with each other. Paul realized that his stepdaughter needed time with her mother so he took his son and stepson out once a week. He accepted Cathy knew best where her daughter was concerned. Cathy began to show her appreciation that Paul had a good relationship with his stepson. Eventually the family was able to move from Cathy's flat into a new place for the new stepfamily where everyone could feel 'at home'. Relationships take time and flash points need strategies. Outside help, such as counselling, either for the couple or family, can ease apparently impossible situations. Helplines are there for instant use. Chapter II will deal more fully with these issues in particular and helplines are listed at the back of the book.

Don't talk about conflict while on the battlefield. Wait until later and then, even if discipline is left to parent and child, the step-parent can talk about how a child's behaviour affects him or her. The step-parent needs a reassuring message when a child who is disturbed by family changes appears to take all the partner's attention.

Patricia, 32, had set up house with her second husband and her four children. She appeared on a late night television programme for about ten minutes talking about the crisis she was experiencing as a new stepfamily. This was her dilemma. 'However much I punish them, they are still naughty and rude. I've rung the social worker because they are so difficult. What can I do?' A panel of experts gave her advice, none of which I remember except that she should contact STEPFAMILY. I found myself thinking about this woman every so often. There were not many facts to go on and Patricia seemed to have done her best – moved house, made an arrangement for regular access and it was all awful. Yet she stayed in my mind, a practical-looking woman, faced by emotional earthquakes which toppled all her sensible plans. What would

I say? Not as an expert, because I'm not, but just as a person who has had time to think rather than produce an instant solution. This is what I came up with:

- Stop punishing for the immediate moment
- Spend an evening a week with your children and without your husband
- Ask them how you can make it easier for them.
- Listen to them
- Tell them you always love them
- Give them a compliment or sign of appreciation every day
- Find a self-help group
- Or do a course, like assertiveness or a Parent Link programme which shows strategies for managing anger, family conflict and rivalry.

The lasting thought those children have is they have lost both parents, their father through separation and their mother to her second husband and, on reflection, Patricia's dilemma illustrated the overwhelming effort that is needed from the mother to make everyone happy. She in turn needs love and support from her husband in order to achieve this, and the effort must also be shared with the father. As Patricia stated the family arrangement was for the children to see their father every fortnight. Phone calls could also give extra contact.

The Boil Of The Family

The frequency of tension between the stepfather and the eldest stepdaughter seems to say this is an impossible relationship, and it is not always the eldest daughter but often the eldest child who has the most to lose emotionally as special companion for the single parent.

Every single parent deserves to remarry and yet the transitions are tough. The needs of parent and child have to be balanced. There are times when all the difficulties seem to erupt in one child, brilliantly described by one man as 'the boil of the family'. An apt image of unseen and unaired poisons bursting out in an unsightly and painful way.

Barbara's husband, Kenny, was very critical of his stepson and at first she joined in seeing her son through her husband's eyes and unaware of how much she had changed in her attitude towards the child. One evening she found nine-year-old Thomas crying in his room: 'He was distraught and said' "Why don't they love me?" I felt so shattered and upset when I heard him. I understood how he felt about the men not loving him; his dad doesn't bother and Kenny was too hard on him.'

His father had moved away from the area and contact with him was not regular and unreliable. The world had fallen apart for Thomas and it had been put together in an alien and uncomfortable way. He could do no right at home and at school he was soon causing trouble and truanting. It took time but Barbara realized Thomas needed attention not criticism, and rather than treat him separately as 'the problem' she spent time with him and worked out ways with Thomas which helped him to settle down at school.

Remember David Copperfield? He was seen by Mr Murdstone, his stepfather, to be in dire need of discipline with a capital 'D'. David became the unwelcome outsider and his beloved mother was a fragile, girlish creature who failed to stand up for her son or herself, deferring instead to the head of the family, as the husband was in Victorian times. David's strict treatment was a complete about turn. He had been his (widowed) mother's support and even her young protector. To be literally, 'a young man' was an admirable way for a boy to behave in those days. But after the appearance of the adult man, the husband, David was sent off to boarding school, conveniently got rid of, and replaced with a new Murdstone baby.

It's easy to say, 'Oh, that's old-fashioned stuff, no-one sends their child away or uses religion to portray a child as wicked.' The modern versions include sending the offending child to therapy or to an educational psychologist or to stay or live with a relative. However sensible these actions may seem they still say, 'this child is a problem, let's single him out from the group show him he's different, push him gently on to the margins.'

Eric is a tall man with an athletic physique yet psychologically he felt terrorized by his six-year-old stepdaughter's wild ways. This gentle giant explained how, although he disagreed with the extreme strictness of his own upbringing by Ghanaian parents, he was caught between his own criteria of child behaviour and his stepdaughter's experience. I'm going to be honest now,' Eric stated, 'and I'm not proud of this but I wanted to get back at her.'

'She used to jump on me, hit me and I would ask her not to. I'd ask her to say "please" and "thank you" and she wouldn't. At first I tried to win her over by persuasion. I know she liked me and she was a lovely child but very naughty. It wasn't her fault, her mother let her get away with murder.

'My father was an accountant and his firm sent him abroad a lot. When he came back he liked to lay down the law which, as a child I didn't feel he had a right to because he wasn't there most of the time. I think western ideas are too liberal and Ghanaian discipline is too harsh, my opinion is in between.'

The way Eric did get back at his stepdaughter was through ignoring her when they were alone. That this was painful was evident because she cried. Eric found himself pushed into a role that he had not chosen. He did not see himself as a parent but describes himself as 'liking children and involved with this child.'

He resented his girlfriend using him as a babysitter. 'She was the going out type, shopping or round to her mother's or with her friends for the evening. It was, "You don't mind, do you?"' *In effect Eric was being given a responsibility for a child he wasn't ready for and did not like to refuse his girlfriend. This couple did separate after three years and Eric's comment was that the relationship ended because they didn't spend enough time as a couple talking and this was the cause of separation, not the child.*

Bad manners does not mean a bad child. Make a clear distinction. If it is your own child that 'acts out the family boil' tell her or him you love them and always will. After all, isn't that what would want to hear from the person who has the power to make life sweet or sour?

Think back to what worked for you as a child. Don't think only in terms of parents and step-parents but the kind of approach taken by adults in your life when you were young and behaving badly.

- What criticism drove you crazy with a sense of unfairness?
- What was your worst punishment as a child?
- Which rules were clear and which unspoken?
- Which adult were you willing to listen to? Why?
- How different in discipline style are you to your parents?

Children change, sometimes bewilderingly. What a six-year-old likes in an adult will not do for a sixteen-year-old. Those children who resist expressions of affection, finding it embarrassing, will still respond to a word of appreciation, an effort to understand them and, perhaps best of all, time set aside for them. That's not just words, that's action.

Marian, with teenage children and stepchildren, insists that she is not going to change her expectations of her children's behaviour even if it doesn't suit Tony, whom she now lives with, but she also expects his children, who visit often, to fit in with her ideas of routine and tidiness. 'That is my side of the household and as Tony is very easygoing he leaves that to me, so although he would do it differently he accepts my way because he's lazy and I'm quite bossy.'

Carol says the same about doing it her way, 'They are my kids and I believe in talking things through and treating them positively. I think Ray's way is too strict and it seems silly to change when I don't want to be like that. In the end they are my responsibility.'

Listening to these mothers I was struck by how definite they were about sticking with their approach to discipline. Their situations are not identical as Carol is taking responsibility for her own children, and Marian for her own plus visiting stepchildren. What they have in common is a decisiveness, a willingness to be frank and strong about the way they feel and what their expectations are. For Carol this meant disagreements with her husband, Ray, who had equally strong ideas, usually the opposite, while Marian established her place in the house by making the house rules and Tony agreed finding this convenient.

The world did not fall apart, their husbands did not condemn them or leave them. It is a difference of opinion, not the judgement between Good and Evil. And I thought back to Barbara and her son, Thomas. She changed to fit in with the stepfather's attitude and it didn't work. However, Marian and Tony agreed on roles while Ray felt an 'outsider' and needed to be considered in family rules.

Inconsistency

It is said time and again how important it is to have a common approach to discipline, to agree and to show the children this united front. If that works, terrific – I'm sure it does for some couples. But how many of us sit down and really talk through what we believe and how to put it into practice? Children have a way of upsetting these neat ideas by having strong ones of their own and there are always those other influences – the main one being the other parent. The stepfamily adults may be busy creating one set of rules but the children have to be flexible enough to cope with two sets.

It isn't easy to create a united front if you are relying on a spontaneous style of agreement between the adults. Look for what you do agree on and build on that. Those will be the things you don't usually think about because they work, the simple – not rules exactly – but agreements, such as no telly while you eat together. Things that are preventative rather than punitive. Inconsistency is almost a capital crime to some adults and children can use this as a way to manipulate the adults but, in other families, it is just natural, human. It is fine to be different from each other and those differences make the adults in the stepfamily attractive and full of interest towards each other. But having totally different attitudes brings confrontation and being totally in agreement can lead to stagnation. Sometimes it seems we have changed our minds. This can be a good thing if it means we are moving on, adapting, changing just as the world does. One thing that doesn't change is that we do care about our children and, as long as that shines through, it will be accepted when we say firmly, 'Yes, I've changed my mind.'

House Rules

Becoming a stepfamily means we have to think about what once came naturally within the family. Several people have to adapt to each others' ways. It can be worrying to start questioning the way we treat the children yet making a new family is another disturbance after the initial one of divorce or separation. Therefore, it is better to cultivate sensible if small actions than endlessly blame the former partner or beat yourself up over what has already happened. We want that new-found love to spill over and heal any hurts the children may have. The children do not always seem that lovable though and sometimes simple house rules help keep the peace.

If your mum has said
No your step Dad might
say yes.

Stella and Larry's children, twelve and nine, drew up their idea of house rules one day. 'The bit about screaming is directed at us, the adults,' she grins. But since the rules seemed very practical Stella set it out on the computer at the college where she's studying and she then displayed it at home. The message relayed was that not only was this fun to make up but also 'they' were taking notice and trying to remember not to be unreasonable too. Notices, however, are notoriously tempting for graffiti additions.

A stepfamily where there seemed to be endless petty arguments initiated 'family meetings' where everyone had an equal say and decisions were agreed. Some of the perennial disputes were settled, at least temporarily, over how much pocket money, at what age and how bedtimes should differ. It was also a chance to feel the satisfaction of power broking for the younger members.

Conflict And Resolution
Towards the children:

- Agree house rules with children
- Prevention is better than punishment
- More action, less words
- Use positive language
  Between partners
- Leave serious discipline to parent
- Parents, don't exclude partner
- When parent isn't there, support their way
- Talk to partner away from children
- Build on agreements, don't focus on disagreements
- Ask for outside help, helplines, counselling, parenting courses or books

Chapter 8

Time together, Time alone

'I married Tessa but I didn't marry the children,' said Robert firmly.

WHEN two people start a relationship they meet in the evenings, spend time talking to each other on the phone and they may go off for a night, a weekend or even on holiday as a couple. They share adult activities – going dancing, to a film, to the pub or for a meal and they talk about adult interests.

Before the commitment of living together, however much time they spend with the children the adults have another separate life together. When you share a home there isn't the same need to go out. The object of your courtship is there beside you.

Robert's statement is so simple and clear. He knows where the boundaries are; where the stepfamily stops. Robert felt secure as a husband because his two young stepchildren already had a set bedtime of 7.30 P.M. He knew the evenings always belonged to them. Many step-parents cannot resist immersing themselves into the new family unit. Whether you are a large or small stepfamily, you will need time with your partner and time apart from the family. You became a step-parent because you married someone who was a parent. That marriage is important and deserves attention. So do you. When you feel confident and relaxed you will be more attentive to your family, noticing, listening and responding in a more positive way. As long as the adults allow time to spend with each other their relationship will tolerate many demands.

Marie says:
'I revelled in my lively, busy household. We played together and did homework together, we baked cakes and made things. It was one big happy family. One big love affair. But the pleasure gradually became a burden I couldn't lay down. We didn't go out that much as a couple, except for parents' evenings – lack of money and lack of energy. Two years after we became a stepfamily we had a baby and the two eldest were in their teens. The children were always there. Late evenings were exhausted silences, sometimes companionable, sometimes not. I wasn't able to resist being there for everyone all the time. I was afraid if I wasn't everything would collapse. Eventually, I saw I had to go out sometimes and it took an interest outside the home to restore me to someone who could have adult conversations again and be someone who could let go.'

All of the family all of the time is too much togetherness. A stepfamily can be quite a tribe when each person brings children to the new relationship. It is just as important though in a small family to make time for the one you did marry. Talk to your partner about bedtimes and if the children are young decide on what kind of evenings you want. Some families enjoy the children's company in the evenings. That's the time when adults relax, especially if both are working, and can appreciate games and cuddles with the children but decide when the children's time stops and when the adults' evening begins. Remember children grow up, then they stay up.

A good babysitting arrangement is essential for a stepfamily. A babysitter whom you and the children know will make for a confident, trouble-free evening out. A babysitter who is needed every week or every fortnight will be reliable. Avoid last minute decisions on who to ask to babysit and avoid taking friends and relations for granted just because they love the children. They will not always be able or want to babysit. Treat your babysitter well and she or he will be a real asset to your stepfamily life.

Feargal's first wife died unexpectedly when their daughter, Alice, was only six years old. She had been living with her mother. It was a traumatic time and their lives changed immediately and dramatically. Feargal's partner says: 'Alice came to live with us and suddenly I was a stepmother in my own home, unprepared. Feargal was very conscious that we needed time on our own. We went out together once a month, not with friends, or to friends, just us. And we had a good babysitting arrangement.' When step-parenting starts with a bereavement the child will need a lot of support and love. These three people were adapting to big changes in their lives and as this was a small family unit there were opportunities for one-to-one attention. Even so, they needed time away from home.

The relationship between the two adults in the family has often been described as the primary one. If this relationship is healthy and happy then the dependent or secondary ones will be too, rather like the roots of a tree which has room to spread into rich, nourishing soil resulting in strong healthy branches.

Even if you do not agree with this analogy – you may feel that the parent and child relationship comes first – it is definitely easier for the children if the adults are happy with each other.

There are ways to create space without going anywhere. If you have a common interest talk about it and share new ideas. Don't always focus on the children or the home. Patrick says 'We realized quite quickly that we needed something that had nothing to do with the children or the household, and we found reading provided that. We chose books that we wanted to talk about and discuss. We had some great conversations and having something objective helped during the times when there seemed to be so many people's feelings to deal with.'

When the stepfamily includes teenage children, or there are children from both parents' previous marriages, home space will be fully occupied. And if there's a baby too, no-one will have much privacy. Children also need individual attention and moments alone with their mother or father.

Some of these times arise naturally such as going to school or bath time, yet your mind may not be with the child or you may be talking to someone else at the same time. Moments together nurture affection and understanding. Children show a different side of their personality when they are on their own and so does a parent. Step-parents who are secure as a husband or wife will be confident enough to resist feeling excluded. In the early, enthusiastic days there may have been a tendency to show care and responsibility by being involved in all the parental activities. You do not need to prove that you are a good step-parent all of the time.

If you are in doubt ask your partner. 'Do you need me to help?' or 'Tell me if you want some time with . . .' Don't be jealous if your husband takes his daughter out. It is an opportunity for you to enjoy some time with your child or another stepchild or simply without anyone at all. Time alone with one stepchild can be the perfect way for seeing his hidden qualities. Doing something that needs a helping hand or sharing an activity takes away any obvious 'I'm trying to like you' approach. Loving your lover's child is not an automatic response and he may not want to show you his best side anyway. Even Groucho Marx was lost for a joke when his daughter refused to be friendly to her stepmother. She had good reason, she had seen quite a few stepmothers, Groucho was married seven times. Still, it is true that second marriages also break down. All the more reason to think through what works for you and what doesn't. Good intentions and past experiences need to be adapted for your stepfamily.

Adults Alone – You won't often be alone together at home, so go out. It does not have to be every week but make it a regular date.

Mother and Child/ren – You need to be together sometimes without any competing loyalties. As a mother you need this as much as your children do.

Father and Child/ren – If the children of your first marriage live with you remember to give and receive undivided attention. If they don't, a phone call is instant contact.

Step-parent and Child – Individual moments create individual bonds.

HOLIDAYS

Stepfamilies who have an absent other parent, whether through death or divorce, will spend every holiday together. Even in a era when each parent is expected to take responsibility there are many who do not or cannot have the children to stay and the ability to value the times the children are happy to spend with friends away from home, will take the strain from the special need these children will have.

Enjoy the times when the children are invited to stay overnight or for a few days with their friends. Naturally, the adults will want to feel confident about whom they visit. Some of these friendships will already have been established before you, as step-parent, appeared in their lives. Their friendships are important and if they have little contact with the other parent, these visits will lessen the feeling that they are missing out on certain activities. In families with stepbrothers and stepsisters from two different families, invitations to stay at a friend's house can offset the comparisons made when one set of children visits the birth parent and the other set has not been able to have such visits.

Many parents have good holiday arrangements worked out at the time of the divorce or separation. It is worth the effort to make sure these are maintained so that the children know what to expect and what to look forward to.

Some parents are inclined to manipulate the power which comes with that custody to suit themselves or make life awkward for the other parent. As a step-parent you have the difficult part of being sympathetic but make sure your partner knows what *you* want. It can be tempting to change plans because something comes up that you want to do together as a family. A special travel discount is on offer or the perfect invitation comes along. Keeping to arrangements agreed by all parties shows respect for everyone concerned and this will bring dividends and flexibility later.

Pamela recognized that her partner wanted to be both parents to his children when they were with him. 'Charlie's first had remarried and she went to live in another country. So they were usually with us in the holidays. But when friends invited them for half-term he said no. They wanted to go. I wanted them to go. But he had to be a perfect dad. We had a bad tempered week all round, not at all restful.'

This over responsible attitude threatened to undermine the very family he cared about and doubling parental care because the mother was so far away was worthy but misplaced. The half-term holiday wasn't much of a refreshing week as no-one really got what they wanted. Encourage your partner to be realistic and trust the children's wishes. It's OK to let go. After one separation most children simply want their remarried parent to be happy and relaxed.

Some step-parents miss the spontaneity of life they had before they entered into a second marriage which came complete with children. Holiday arrangements now involve many considerations and circumstances change, people move house or get a job somewhere else. Not all families choose the regular option, where stepchildren know who they will be seeing and when. Not all families have a choice. You may have uncertainty thrust upon you. It maybe a case of, 'Is he going to have the children this summer?' or 'When is she going to have the children?'

Whether holidays are shared equally or not they have to be discussed with the other parent. As a step-parent you will have your preferences and can talk it over with partner and children.

However, as the children get older they have a right to some choice as to how and where they wish to spend holiday time. After years of caring for a stepchild, the most understanding adult can feel left out when a teenager decides to spend more holiday time with the other parent. A good relationship between a child and his or her natural parent is good for everyone but not always easy to see. It can work the other way too. Adolescent activities may take up weekends and holidays that have to be spent away from the parent. 'Tell dad I can't come I've got football, ice skating or paid babysitting, or a dance or even homework.' That can be misunderstood by the other parent who has been used to regular visits and who may well find himself missing the weekends with his children.

Dan and Michael lived with their dad and his wife and her older son. When they were fourteen and fifteen sports became a priority. Their mother felt hurt they did not want to come from Derbyshire to London every fortnight. It had been a regular arrangement, now all the adults were put out by the adolescents wanting to make their own decisions. The mother had moments of being completely distraught, angry and felt treated badly. Arrangements were cancelled at very short notice or even sent via a message. At the same time as wanting to insist the boys behave like responsible adults Jane felt like a rejected child herself and was terrified of showing her sons this. She wanted to blame the father although after talking it over with friends she realized that this happens in all families. Young people want to do their own thing and they do not know the old emotions it unleashes in parents and it is not their problem.

This was a rocky moment with old arguments and suspicions coming up between the mother and father. Inevitably this affects the step-parent practically and psychologically and, instead of a fortnightly break, there were extra emotions and lots of muddy boots and dirty washing but because access had worked in the past this turned out to be a small break in the trust that had been built up.

A child can be lucky enough to have two loving families to spend time with during the holiday. However fair arrangements seem to be to the adults some children may feel it just is not what they want. What Dan and Michael wanted did not seem fair to the adults but, after a few months, they settled down to more weekends at home, with extra holiday time with their mother as well as more phone calls and at sixteen London was very attractive for the latest fashion.

Your holiday checklist should include the following points:

- plan ahead
- consult before decisions
- choice for older children
- let everyone know

Happy Christmas? Happy Birthday?

There are special events in the year which bring extra expectations of love and harmony. These are often times of intense pressure and reminders of broken relationships or of previous happy times. Birthdays and Christmas are annual events which have a special significance for the parent and child relationship. Negotiated arrangements need to be respected and the step-parents and half-siblings accommodated. It can be a lot of work, not least emotionally, and Christmas can carry an unrealistic image of family togetherness.

The simplest arrangements are often the best. If parents live in the same area then alternating Christmas Day and Boxing Day or New Year is the obvious one. If not, travel can be complicated and be an added expense.

A couple each had a son of seven-years-old from a previous marriage. Her son lived with them and his son lived with the first wife. 'We tried alternating but it seemed tricky and after a while the most natural way seemed for each child to spend Christmas with his mother. That was fine because I saw my son other times and then Christmas wasn't so loaded.' However, the alternating Christmas is the most popular way and every other year can bring an opportunity for added enjoyment. However, for Shelley the Christmas arrangements are different. 'I have Chris and the baby and we won't have another child so having his two older ones makes it really fun. We get the chance to do all those Christmassy things, play games, lots of presents and the baby loves all the attention and noise. The other year we do the opposite and visit parents and get spoilt in our turn. I certainly wouldn't like either every year it wouldn't be so relaxed.'

Other families long for Christmas to be perfect and happy for the children. However, in practice, Christmas time may bring out the worst if there are problems which have not been aired or resentments which remain unhealed. 'It would have been impossible to say what I wanted because my parents weren't friends. We did alternate between two stepfamilies and at my father's there was an unspoken rule not to talk about my mother so at Christmas and birthdays I had to be careful what I said. There was pressure not to like too much what my mother's husband gave me as well,' confesses Rick. Other children can say wonderfully frank things like, 'My stepmother gives me really great presents so I like going there.' Or 'It's so many people when my stepdad's kids come we can make a lot of noise and no-one minds.'

Good arrangements throughout the year takes away the pressure from Christmas. If Christmas is a crisis then there could be something simmering all year. Whatever this may be, Christmas provides the opportunity for it to surface and, in spite of Christmas being the time for peace and goodwill, it is not the best time to deal with sensitive feelings.

At least there is only one Christmas a year. Birthdays too are once a year but one for each child. This day may be a day of attention and presents, it is also the anniversary of that child's birth. In a tolerant and secure family that child now has the love and appreciation of a step-parent too. Let your stepchild know his or her parent is not excluded by appreciating the parent's present and making it uncomplicated for child and parent to be in touch with a phonecall.

It may be your partner who takes the responsibility for birthdays. Your partner may also feel threatened or vulnerable or even torn between several needs. Talk about the choices available without the child present first so that you can express any worries. Don't have unrealistic expectations of yourself. It is a rare family where the step-parent can genuinely invite a parent and not have some competitive or critical feeling. Certainly it is not impossible but if this is how you feel, however politely hidden your feelings are, you will be putting a strain on yourself and, consequently, on others. Think first, how can you make your gesture of goodwill and then let them have the foreground.

Whether it is holidays, Christmas or birthdays, remember some children do not want the emotional burden of openly choosing whom to spend time with. If there is a choice, talk it through with your partner first. Then decide how much to leave to your partner and your stepchild. Decisions do affect the step-parent but if you are satisfied with the way they are made, then you will be able to accept the decisions themselves. Even though Christmas is always a focal point for families whatever age, all children, even step-children, grow up soon enough and arrange their own celebrations and holidays. One day they may well be inviting you to visit them.

Christmas Experiences

- The children go to their dad, we have a romantic time on our own
- He spoilt our day when his kids went to their mother
- It's best when all the children are together
- He goes to his first wife and children, I feel miserable
- The children like us all to have Christmas dinner together, my children, their dad, his partner and their half-sister

Chapter 9
Children Talking

*The first time I saw my Tio Ramon I thought my mother was playing a joke. **That** was the prince she had been sighing over? I had never seen such an ugly man. That night my bed was transferred to the ironing room. I still did not realize that something basic had changed in the family order.*

'Paula' by Isabel Allende

IN WANTING to be a good enough step-parent or in being lost in a new love, the children's views may get lost. The adults know best. But research findings have shown a difference in how children and adults viewed the same stepfamily situation. It is tough to try and do things in the best possible way and then find out you had completely the wrong idea in the first place. What would you see through a child's eyes? This chapter attempts to show their points of view. Some of the voices in this chapter are talking about their past and a few are talking about what's happening now. But many stepchildren can't put into words what they experience because of loyalty and the inarticulateness of youth, although very young children can be remarkably frank and quite often at very inconvenient moments. 'What I want is, I want to live with all my family in our old house, Mummy,' a three-year-old stated. The fact that his father now lived somewhere else with a new partner was irrelevant to this wish. His mother repeated this to his father, partly because in her heart that's what she would have liked, maybe that's why his father refused to believe a child of three could express himself so clearly. If that child could not have what he wanted, his wish could have been a starting point for more contact instead of being ignored.

I heard similar stories where a child spoke in such a straight-forward and practical way that the listening parent, repeated them, but was not believed. Adults generally prefer to talk *about* children and their well-being rather than actually ask them questions and listen to their answers because they are so afraid they will not be able to give them what they ask for. Children may say what will be too painful for the adult to hear. How do we get the balance right between talking openly and finding out the children's opinions without putting adult responsibilities and choices onto their shoulders?

Putting It Into Words

We all want to be noticed and our feelings taken seriously and a few words can make huge differences. Three-year-old Paul's statement could have reminded the father to say, for example, 'I still want you to come and stay with me.' Children talk with striking simplicity about adult behaviour which is at odds with how they, the children feel. Some of these situations or events lie in the memory and affect their happiness like small stones in a shoe.

'I still remember how much it annoyed me when my stepdad used to walk through the kitchen at breakfast time and just switch off the radio. He didn't even say anything to us.' Trina was the youngest of three, all of whom are now adults in their twenties and thirties. As children they lived in the Welsh countryside with their mother, her husband and a half-brother and they often stayed with their father who lived nearby with his wife.

'I didn't think of him as my stepfather but he had this air of the man of the house so I never felt able to object to things I didn't like.' Switching off the radio may seem a minor action, and in another family it would be, but to Trina it said everything about how he ignored the children but silently imposed his will on the household. Both Paul's statement and Trina's story illustrate the powerlessness that the children felt. The younger child could not have said what he wanted more clearly. Nine-year-old Trina had already given up saying anything. Now at twenty-five, she still feels a distance between her and her stepfather although she acknowledges that he has changed a lot and believes that if she needed help or advice he would willingly give it.

Kept Out

Trina's observation, 'We used to get into bed with dad and Katie but never with Tim and mum,' demonstrates how powerful unspoken boundaries can be. Not all children remain quiet, as adults know and despair over at times. Children can be angry, cruel, manipulative, even mentally disturbed. However, they are still children. Even if they are not encouraged to articulate their feelings, these feelings will be 'acted out'. Even the most laidback, streetwise urban youth who can make his presence felt does not always find it easy to tell the right person exactly what bothers him. Owen and his sister lived with his father and stepmother in north London.

'I used to have huge rows with my stepmother. We just didn't get on. I could see she spent more money on clothes and Christmas presents for her kids (girls) and my sister doesn't say much so I felt angry at the way she was treated. I could see she didn't get what the others got. My dad was an easygoing bloke and, although he earned the money, my stepmother spent it and I minded that we didn't get treated the same. My dad would never say anything.' Now Owen has grown up he is 21, and left home, he and his stepmother get on better, 'I do like her especially when we're having a drink. In that situation we're different.' Perhaps this has something to do with being adults and on equal terms, away from the tense relationship of stepmother and stepchild. However, when he talks about the past Owen brings up the old hurts regardless of his friendly, frank comments about the present and, though he says he likes her, the stepmother is blamed. 'I used to get kicked out, it was her running the house. My dad just took the easy way out, I would have liked it if he had made an effort.' Owen seems to accept that his father's first loyalty has been transferred to his new wife and family or that there was some division of roles, i.e. the man earned the money and the woman spent it and therefore his father has done his part. In both Trina's and in Owen's stories the parent either does not know about the situation or appears to take a back seat and relinquish responsibility in the domestic arena. It is inevitable that parents do not always know what's happening between their partner and their child and, anyway, they do not always want to interfere.

Talking And listening

If you want your child to get on with your partner then you must realize that it will not be smooth at all times and, in cultivating trust and equality, you will have to step back sometimes. So, how do you achieve a balance and leave the way open to allow the children to tell you difficult things or to complain about you or your favourite adult.

- Find a way to encourage grouses and serious worries to be put into words
- Find a time to listen so that the child can get it off her mind
- Make it clear when you can and can't do something to solve the problem
- Make it clear when you will try anyway

Is it clear to your child when it is safe to bring up things that he would not want said openly in the family? No parent can work miracles or change other people or their attitudes but listening and trying helps. Keep it simple if you do offer to try and change something. Resist turning a clear insight into a complicated conversation. I have seen a mother respond with a flood of explanations and reassurances to a teenage son who said in a few honest words, 'I don't feel wanted round at my dad's. It hurts me a lot that my dad's wife doesn't like me.' I was impressed by how much he understood himself and that he did not have any reserve, or self-pity, about saying this while his stepdad and his mum were there. He may have regretted expressing himself this way as it set loose a tirade from his mum who felt she needed to make everything all right.

When I asked Stuart, 17, for a few words on what was good about being a stepfamily it was 'having a man around' – Stuart has two older sisters – and 'we talk about football' (football can make for brilliant bonding) and the fact that he had acquired step-brothers, 'I always wanted brothers and I get on really well with them; they come and stay here, we camp in the garden and I go round there and I get on with their mother too.'

How many situations do you remember as a child where the adults, those all-powerful beings who kept telling you what was what and how much better they knew about everything, actually did not seem to notice what was really going on? When it is a stepfamily this lack of observation becomes that much more complicated.

'I couldn't understand why mum didn't stand up for me? Why did she agree with him?' Mum actually had no idea how her daughter felt. Children think their parents know or should know. How can they not know? In a busy family life, where there are many people and demands, it may not be possible to create space where spontaneous confidences can happen. And planned times, when a child knows that if there is anything to say it will be heard and, just as important, when you can ask them how they are.

Two Parents, Two Homes

When talking is encouraged or the child is old and confident enough to initiate conversations, the build-up of resentments and crises can be avoided. 'I'm very close to my dad and if there's anything bothering me I usually do talk to him, I can tell him anything.' Kelly is sixteen and lives in London, her parents separated eight years ago and remain friendly, living near to each other. Since the separation Kelly and her younger brother have spent alternate weeks with each parent and see the way that their parents co-operate in looking after them. Four years ago Kelly's father met Sandra and so one of their two homes has changed.

My Homes

The experience of shared care of the children has meant that the two parents had to talk to each other and keep up a domestic relationship. Both parents knew the daily concerns of the children and spent equal amounts of time with the children. Then along came Sandra. 'I don't find it easy to tell Sandra what I think. I didn't like it when she used my room like a storeroom.' This was Kelly's territory at her father's house before her stepmother moved in. Kelly accepts the differences that come with having a stepfamily. She is glad that her father is happy and she loves her younger half-sister, and she is old enough to see and put into words the differences between adult and children's views. 'I don't think of her as a stepmother although I do say my stepmum. I think of her as my dad's wife or Abby's Mum (Abby is Kelly's half-sister). I think she likes to see us as sisters but I don't think we're close enough.' This is a graphic description of how the child acknowledges the step-parent's wish to be close to her and how the stepchild views the relationship in a more detached, realistic way. Kelly continues with a low key but genuine statement, 'I like her, but there are lots of things I don't like about her way of living.' and one of them is Sandra's untidiness and hence the quick solution of stuffing the overflow into Kelly's room which, from her point of view, is not used every day. Kelly is still at school, a shy and quiet person and being the eldest she has a special bond with her own mother who has remained single.

Nowadays it is no longer unusual for two separated or divorced parents to want to agree about caring equally for the children. It is also no longer unusual for a father to want to stay nearer to his children and make it possible for them to remain part of his life. In Kelly's situation the parents have shared decisions equally and Kelly had roots in each home with her own room and possessions. But how do the children feel moving between two homes?

Helen, seventeen, has her own room in her father's house, her brother shares a room with his step-brother. They feel that their main home is with their mother because they spend more time there, have more friendship links in the neighbourhood and go to school from there. Nevertheless, the visited home has an acknowledged space that is their own, but the house rules are different which detracts from it ever feeling as homely. 'That's fine because we have a good time there and I am very close to my father. It's being with him that's the main thing that I want', Helen explains. Kelly is more reflective. 'I act differently at each house, I'm quieter there, (her dad and step-mother's) and here (mum's) I can be my mad self. There I want to show how mature I am. It's a way of getting respect. Wherever you are, your own parents know you're one person'.

How sensitive are we to spoken or unspoken criticism? Are we confident with the ability to laugh at ourselves and be tolerant or even consider a change might be in order? Our society has come a long way since shame and humiliation was attached to a child of divorced or unmarried parents, and even when a second nuclear family was recreated, secrets were created alongside it. How hard it must have been for parents, especially those who were attempting to create a new, happier family, to see the effects of these secrets on the children.

The Stepfamily Child

Georgina is 47 years old and lives in Wales. She grew up in the fifties and her mother, a widow with two children married a divorced man with two children who visited him. Georgina is the child of the second relationship, the stepfamily, but she was born before the actual marriage. She was not a stepchild but was a half-sister in a stepfamily. Even so she suffered the intolerance that was showered on any family marked by divorce, separation, illegitimacy and remarriage. 'The feeling that I was in some way unworthy, haunted me for a great deal of my life.' A second marriage was not a straightforward event when divorce was hard to obtain and was accompanied by such prejudice. No wonder that many children were born before the second marriage could take place, now at least much of the stigma of illegitimacy has gone. Georgina's story highlights the fact that the child of a stepfamily is also aware of the feelings swirling about within that family unit. More stepfamilies than not have a child in the new relationship. And as the numbers of second marriages rise there are many who have been through the kind of experience described above and then themselves become step-parents.

Presents Giving And Getting

Kim was strongly motivated by her own stepfamily circumstances to do better when she became a stepmother. 'I really thought about how I wanted to be from the beginning because I had been in a stepfamily. It gave me high expectations of what I wanted from myself. What I hated was my father leaving things like buying presents to his wife. We got feminine presents after he remarried so we knew it was her who had bought them.'

The giving of presents is loaded with signals and messages. Through advertising and, therefore, through children's expectations, the giving and costs of presents have become a burden for parents.

However old the stepchildren are, the signals and messages conveyed behind their presents have stayed in their minds and is frequently mentioned as an action that still causes them pain. Such as the fact it was the stepmother who chose and bought the father's gift for his child, and deciding how much to spend on it. What is a son or daughter worth in money and effort? The child sums it up in a glance. The message is make that extra effort whoever you are in the stepfamily. When you buy a present and you're not sure what to get, just ask. The children will probably tell you before you ask if given half a chance. Listen first. It is perfectly reasonable to say that certain things are too expensive, and ask if there is something else they want or say you'll go that extra mile to get something similar. Take them shopping and you might be shocked at how much consumer goods aimed at the children's presents market actually are. Negotiate on cost, check what the other parents spend, you may possibly even enjoy it. That must be better than an unwanted gift that says 'can't be bothered'.

Attention Giving And Getting

Martin at eighteen says one of the nicest times is when he and his stepfather of thirteen years go out together for a quiet beer. 'We do get on anyway, I see him as a guardian rather than a stepfather. If we're both at home he's working or I'm in my room with friends. So it's nice to leave the house. He is more approachable out and I get lots of attention. I go for a drink just with my mum too. I have a lot of respect for him, I know how much he's done for me.'

Getting attention is a big issue and children are forced to use quite complicated ways and means to get what they need if that attention is not on offer. What exactly is this attention seeking anyway? Do we all crave it or despise it? Attention seeking used to describe any action the speaker disapproved of; showing off was another word to show disapproval; acting out is the latest description used by those who analyze family dynamics. Tummy aches and other minor, sometimes major, illnesses are popular means of seeking attention as are 'carelessness', showing off, 'temper tantrums', stealing and being a goody goody. 'Parents should spend time with their children. That's what I want, just on my own with my mum, because now I don't get as much attention and sometimes you should all go out and do something nice for the children,' explains John, eleven, who now shares his mum with stepfather, visiting stepsister and half-brother. Hilary visited her mother for several weeks once a year as her parents lived so far away from each other. 'I felt her husband was so competitive and jealous of me. Mum was so busy doing everything, it took a while before I could get some of her attention. I would always get ill after a few days. The worst thing was that she didn't realize how much I wanted her to notice me.'

'Instead I think she avoided being with one person and maybe causing jealousy by always being busy. It seemed easier for her to do some cooking or be the one who looked after the whole household and, as it was miles from anywhere, there was always loads to do to keep the place running.'

The roles begin to change when a child becomes an adult, 'It used to take a week for us to feel natural. Now I can see her insecurities and she is so much more relaxed and says "Oh, is that the right present that you wanted?" and wants to know if everything's all right.'

However infrequently these adults see each other in later life, the ties and bonds of the stepmother or stepfather relationship will remain. Simon in his late forties, sent a card to friends declining an invitation saying he was going to visit his stepmother as she was getting on and he had not seen her for some time. Similarly Anna, in her fifties, whose life has been tied up lately with her stepfather's illness.

We are aware of our parents' and stepparents' needs as they get older and become frailer. But do we give that 'step' name to anyone married to a parent? Is it more likely to be 'my father's wife' or my mother's 'husband'. Surprisingly often, even if the marriage is long after the children have grown and left.

What The Children Say To Step-Parent And Parent

- Talk to us, don't just do things first
- Don't interrupt
- Listen
- Ask questions
- Don't criticize the parent
- Don't think you're perfect
- Treat each child equally but not the same
- Don't be too lenient or too hard.
- Try to stay out of conflicts between parent and child
- Have time for the children
- Do something with the children that they choose

Chapter 10

The parent who doesn't live with the children

At FIRST I called this chapter 'the absent parent' but I was struck with the phrase one offended and impassioned father used, 'I'm the parent who doesn't live with the children.' The word 'absent' can have rather a pejorative connotation, as if all parents who did not live with their children had consciously decided to absent themselves. And I couldn't see that parent's view if I thought of him, and sometimes her, as absent, in the distance. Of course some step parents will also have children and will be trying to keep in touch with the everyday lives of their own children living elsewhere.

It doesn't automatically follow that separation means that the other parent is in a wounded state. The other parents are a mixed bunch like the rest of the world, some have satisfactory lives and goodwill, some feel devastated by the break-up, some have moved to a remote Scottish island or taken a job in Saudi Arabia, some have disappeared into the sunset, many live down the road and share parenting, some remain good friends, some feel ignored, some are poor, some well-off. Most will have another adult in their life, although not necessarily making a joint household.

A PLACE FOR THE OTHER PARENT

The natural parent wants to know where he fits in relationship to his children. I say he because it is more often the father, just as there are more stepfathers there are more fathers who do not live with their children. It used to be accepted, if not acceptable, that the father should go off and be erratic about keeping in touch. It was certainly in keeping with the old practices of the father going out to work and having less affectionate contact and day to day care with the children. Values have changed and, together with the pressure to provide equal financial support, the parent, man or woman, whether in a stepfamily of their own or not, expects to play a part in the child's life. There is plenty of catching up with the new vision.

Hopes	Fears
● Regular contact	● Irregular contact
● Share information	● Find out by chance
● Regular maintenance	● Late/arguments over money
● Co-operation	● Battles over access
● Friendly attitude	● Defensive/manipulative
● Clear boundaries	● Confusion and change

Tony is a gentleman in a modern sense. He is gentle, creative and enjoys the company of women. He has a ponytail and bleaches his hair to keep it blonde and in the competitive world of the capital city he is often but not endemically out of work as a freelance sub-editor on popular magazines.

Adam and Alice, Tony's son and daughter, are in their late teens. Their main home is in Devon with their mother when they are not away at college. So phone calls are the most frequent contact.

'Adam will just drop into the conversation, "love you lots". When they were little I didn't like all this daddy one and daddy two business, (father and stepfather). I couldn't handle that so I stood back and let them get on with their new life. So I'm Tony, which is fine. But I was always around.'

Tony remained on friendly terms with his ex-wife (he was the unwilling person in the separation) and these were enhanced, naturally enough, when the stepdad left the scene. Tony and his ex-wife had even considered getting back together. 'The ironic thing was the other children (the younger half-brother and half-sister) asked me if I would be their daddy too.' *It is easy to see the mixture of needs and emotions and their attempts at keeping in touch. Tony's point of view is that he preferred to withdraw rather than accept relegation to the daddy role.*

Freedom or Feeling Excluded

I know as a stepmother and mother the frustrations I've felt towards the two absent parents because I couldn't see what they saw or understood what their thoughts were. I saw them as being somehow more powerful than me and this may not be what your experience is. However, this changed when we talked or saw each other and I stopped being so defensive or feeling I had to prove something or show how brilliantly I coped, even if I did not see myself doing this.

When I listened to Tony I saw for the first time how someone could feel excluded and perhaps feel not worthy enough to take some action to change this. Before, I had seen the other parent as the one who, not exactly as the one who got away, but the one who was not working hard, who had kept some personal freedom and who had not dropped an interesting mind for the dirty washing. I saw the parent as unwilling to be supportive when the children still needed two parents to care for them and show the care with money and time because my experience of doing without much help was the norm for me.

Jeremy lives in a village in Buckingham. He works very hard as a self-employed carpenter and just about keeps on top of life financially and in spite of this has the energy and satisfaction of a man who likes his work. His ex-wife and child moved to Bristol and are part of a stepfamily. Twelve-year-old Lauren has two stepsisters and, after the first difficult year, everyone got on well and have cultivated friendly contact.

'I didn't know that Lauren gave Terry a hard time in the beginning but I think it was also the moving and being uprooted which upset her. They get on fine now, he's a nice guy.'

Jeremy spends a lot of time agonizing about whether he should move because he doesn't feel as if he sees his daughter often enough. In fact, he thinks around this problem all the time, but in the end nothing has changed. He talks about 'quality time' as if it doesn't happen and yet could. His work commitments conflict with other commitments not only with his child, but also with the woman in his life who lives in London with her children.

'I feel as if I should move nearer to Lauren but then I would have to start all over again with work contacts. One big reason that keeps me here is because Lauren is such good friends with Polly who lives in this house. So Lauren gets me and to see her great friend whom she's known since they were babies. In the end I give up working out a better way. 'But that doesn't stop me feeling guilty and thinking "she's growing up and I should be there for her more than I am." I notice I can be a recluse and get on with work and find myself not even thinking of her. When my mother was old and needed me I regretted moving to Buckingham and felt I should have moved to Kent to be near her.'

Quality Contact

What Jeremy does provide is the home that Lauren has always known, her other family home with the bonus of her friend. Her father's friends are around and she sees him in his world where he feels confident and, apart from the guilt tendency, good about himself. He rings her up from time to time rather than having fixed phone call arrangements. He has Lauren during the holidays, often combining it with camping with other family friends and is happy for stepsister, Rowan to come too. 'They go off and I'll get a big hug in passing and then suddenly they're gone again. Or, if she's feeling miserable about something she will come and ask me to put her to bed or she'll sit on my lap and be my baby, and ask me for attention.'

Even at home Jeremy feels he wants 'quality time' with Lauren partly because it is so easy for his daughter to spend more time with her friend than her dad and partly because he does not have that much 'quality time' himself. The house where he lives is shared and he does not feel at home there any more. Of course it is easy for him to retreat into his work when his daughter's stepfamily home is such a distance.

'I am a long distance parent. Parents can drive, children can't. They have to wait for us to make our way to them.' It is a strange fact that it is easy to spend hours on the phone to people we see often and already have a good connection with. So why don't parent and children have plenty of what Jeremy called electronic hugs and telephonic kisses? Perhaps Jeremy lacks the confidence to know when he's doing well. At a recent household party, he didn't find it unusual that he invited his daughter's family. Lauren was there having a great time with her friends as were her stepsisters, his former wife and her husband.

It Makes Life Easier if you:

- Stay friends with your ex-partner
- Respect time between child and other parent
- Encourage regular phone calls both ways

How can one survive when the new family pattern isn't doing well? Jim sees his children in his old home, in a new family, a stepfamily with his ex-wife and her boyfriend and is distraught. 'I have some amazing friends who help me through the worst times. It has been so bad but when I see the children it's fine. I have been through loss through death and that is nothing as terrible as being hurt as a parent, undermined overtly and covertly. It could have been alright but it seems she just wants to wipe me out. It's only in the last few months I can take on board the idea that my relationship with the children can endure even if I don't see them very often.'

Separation And Loss

Jim was married for fourteen years and didn't want to leave his wife or his four children. He said his wife did not want to live with him anymore and thought of leaving him in the home with the children. They had talked about shared parenting, each having equal time with and responsibility for the children. Anyone who has been a parent at all, and for Jim it was thirteen years, will not only suffer from the end of a marriage but will also suffer an unpleasant transition from the parent they wanted to be to a parent they did not choose to be. You cannot let go of parenting as if it was a discarded skin or a natural cycle in life like children leaving home. Parents have needs and they need the children as well as the other way round. Perhaps it is true that adults have ways of coping and are not dependent but there is a fundamental human need to exercise the love one has for one's offspring. If there is not a channel for this love then there is pain or numbness or anger. It was with this understanding of joint care that Jim agreed, reluctantly, to leave. Only later did the pain hit home, realizing it was not going to be quite like the idea agreed. 'I was about the most committed father, as fully involved as you could imagine, changing nappies, taking the children to school, cooking and housework. I feel she used her power to oust me. She's horrible.' Jim settled into a new home only six miles away, large enough for the children as well and, for the last few years, he has been sharing this with his girl friend. Jim charts the decline from joint care and open contact to angry confrontations with threats. 'First she didn't want me coming to the house then she refused when they wanted to stay the night with me. My son stayed one night after football training which is nearer to me and her boyfriend came and banged on the door shouting. Her response causes anxiety in the children who don't want to upset her. She gets hysterical and I stay relatively calm so it appears to the children that I upset her.' Typically, it is impossible to know all the rights and wrongs of this impasse but many ex-partners will identify with the hurt of being excluded and angrily cast out and treated like the devil, a monster, an unwanted intruder to be kept away from the fragile building of the new stepfamily.

To the parent who does not live with the children it is the injustice of it all that hurts, missing out and not having an active role in the children's growing up. Jim also feels damaged by what he sees as the advantage women have, 'If the mother wants to obstruct she has all the weight of the law. It's a crucial time when women have more power and it's tempting to misuse it'. That is Jim's view based partly on his experience of being cut out.

When opposing views cause such distress, mediation can help ex-partners to agree some basic points of good parenting behaviour.

It Makes Life Easier if you are:

- Living within easy travelling distance
- Friends staying supportive without judging
- Making sure children can tell you what's wrong without feeling disloyal
- Willing to use mediation services (see details at the end of this chapter)

It can be tempting for the parent in the step-family to flaunt the supposed perfection of a new happy stephome at the ex-partner. Pamela remembers being told by her ex-husband how everything had now worked out perfectly. It was many years later that the second wife heard this and was astonished as she had suffered from feeling compared to a more exciting (if ultimately destructive) first love.

> *Sarah went to great lengths to make sure she was not cut out of her twin sons' growing up. When she was upset for not getting their school reports (they automatically went to the boys' father as the boys lived with him) she asked the school directly for them and from then on sent she sent a stamped addressed envelope to the school for her copy. As the boys grew older she received the kind of feedback that comes from each parent having different things to offer their children just as if they were still together.*
>
> *Sarah was good at getting information and organizing which came in useful when they needed books and reference material for homework assignments and preparing for GCSEs and she loved planning weekends with them in the city where such good facilities existed like swimming pools and tennis courts. The hiccups occurred and self-doubts began to manifest themselves when, as teenagers, the boys just wanted to hang-out and not do anything much. Although there was criticism between the mother*

and the father, Sarah had no such problems with his partner. 'I respected what she did right from the beginning when she and Bernard got together and the boys were three years old.' *Sarah spoke admiringly about her twin sons' stepmother, Fiona, whom she described as taking on ex-husband, Bernard and the boys and giving them stability.* 'I felt slightly in awe of her as she was absolutely clear she wouldn't buy into my pain and made sure Bernard didn't opt out of being the parent. It was Fiona who decided they should move from the city to the country and she created a family. She did a hell of a lot. And as she wasn't tremendously maternal, I could be and in a sense we were complementary.'

Sarah lives on her own and works as an advertising sales manager. Her earnings are good but this fluctuates with seasonal variations. When arguments arose with her ex-husband over money for the children's fares she rearranged payment by buying the tickets through an agent in the boys' home town. Before they were old enough to travel without an adult she says, 'I religiously commuted one hour to collect them from Bernard at the station and bring them back to stay with me. I did this every fortnight, Friday till Sunday. I believe in establishing ground rules and sticking to them come hell or high water. Then everyone knows it can't be swayed.'

Clear Roles

Much of these regular arrangements were down to her persever-ance but she appreciates that everything was aided by Fiona's insistence that Bernard was always responsible for co-operating with Sarah, not her as stepmother. Bernard brought the boys to the station to meet their mother.

There were rocky moments when Sarah felt left out or bereft of a part to play in her sons' lives. She strived to resist the feeling of being no use to her own children and tried to hold on to the rational thought that this moment would pass. She knows that all parents have doubts about their worth.

It's just hard to remember that the doubts and feelings of being excluded from the supposedly happy stepfamily are at the bottom of a multitude of unresolvable situations. The stepfamily may only see the smart career woman and be misled by the energetic professional attitude. If that other parent does not have a second family and enjoys a job or career she or he may forget that family life cannot be planned and managed as can some other parts of life.

It makes life easier if:

- Separate relationships with school are kept
- The birth parent has direct arrangements with older children
- You stick to ground rules
- Be as pleasant as possible

'When I first went for a job interview they asked me if I had children and I told them they didn't live with me. I felt awful as if I had a great big sign sticking up – GUILTY.' *Patricia's daughter eventually came to live with her mother at the age of fourteen.*

Her son moved in soon after so he could go to college in London. Before that there were eleven years when the children lived with their father. And although she had regular access and went to Gloucestershire to visit every fortnight it was a very painful and devastating separation.

'It did make an awful mark on me, it was a terrible thing at the time. But it's like someone with a broken leg, you have to get on with it. I left for someone else and my husband went for divorce and got care and custody. The children were four and seven.'

'I used to go down to see the teachers at their school. I couldn't get to parents evenings or the open days but they appreciate a parent who takes an interest so I could ring and go when I wasn't working. He did get married again and they had a stepmother and a stepbrother and stepsister more or less the same age as them. My kids speak to them on the phone sometimes. I know they don't like their stepmother because that's why my daughter came to live with me, it got too difficult for her father.'

The traumatic separation from her children and later, when her ex-husband remarried Patricia was refused access to the house, could have led to a crisis. How was she to see the children? Fortunately, a friend offered her a place to stay with the children in a nearby town.

Both Sarah and Patricia belong to MATCH, Mothers Apart from their Children, and the support and networking as above healed some of the doubts and fears and restored some confidence in themselves as parents. Now they value the changes they see in themselves and others in similar positions. In the beginning it was hard to see that anything would change. It is worth remembering for all parents and stepparents that, 'Our children do grow up and get a voice of their own.'

Disapproval And Distress

There is still a terrible stigma attached to the mother who, for whatever reason does not live with her children. Social disapproval is powerful and punishing stuff. It causes great distress and uncertainty for mothers and children.

The majority of mothers who live apart from their children do so not through choice but because of a difficult event or situation. This can be illness, money, postnatal depression, or being the partner who decided the marriage was at an end. However, responsibility for the children is changing from a strictly either or situation to a shared care attitude and more families can now make a decision based on what is most practical or best for the children or have a mutual agreement that the children live with their father.

If the parents are in agreement then the mother can have confidence in her new role as a different but equally worthwhile parent. However, the social stigma towards mothers living away from their children still exists even if society finds it acceptable for men to leave the home and children. There is a historical difference in attitude towards fathers and mothers who leave the family unit and that is carried around in our sub-conscious. Although now a discarded preliminary to divorce proceedings the guilty party still exists. Feelings and attitudes do not easily submit to new ideas or logic. Moral judgements, however rarely mentioned out loud, end up worrying the children and may affect their natural relationship with the other parent. If the stepfamily can allow even a small bit of understanding towards the parent who does not live with the children that will help. You have your roles and have made your choices in the stepfamily but seeing another person's situation from their perspective can soften feelings of tension and opposition.

The Other Parents' Views

What fathers say:
- I'm an errant father with little money and little time.
- I'm a long distance father. Parents can drive, children can't
- In this society the father is an assistant at best.
- The resident parent has the power and it's tempting to misuse it.

What mothers say:
- I felt guilty if anyone asked if had children.
- Fathers send them back quickly enough when adolescence strikes
- I want to give things I choose, not money
- I would go without to pay for the train fare. Women still earn less.

Checklist
Who do you recognize Tony, Jeremy, Jim, Sarah, Jackie?
Note down the big issues for you and your stepfamily
e.g. quality time, feeling excluded, feeling blamed, money, co-parenting, access, travel arrangements

National Family Mediation
9 Tavistock Place, London WC1H 9SN
Tel: 0171 383 5993
Scotland: 0131 220 1610

Chapter 11

Help And Inspiration

Getting support

Being a good enough parent is not automatic yet many of us behave as if it must be some personal lack in us when all is not well with the rest of the family. In a stepfamily doubts of our ability and worth are magnified. If you are giving yourself a hard time or you feel irrational anger or guilt or just wonder why the hell you wanted to be part of a stepfamily then there are all kinds of useful, practical and even enjoyable ways to help yourself.

Step back and take some time out, take advantage of the many support organizations and self-help groups. Use them to meet others in similar situations, exchange views and experiences. Rediscover yourself as an individual and the good parts unique to your stepfamily. 'At least we never argue over that!' or 'We're lucky with grandparents and step grandparents. They wish us well and stay in touch.'

The variety of helpful options is enormous, just like step families, and what suits you may not be the obvious or the same as your friend or neighbour. Therefore this chapter includes what has worked for some people to give you plenty of ideas and inspiration on what could work for you.

Self-Help
The effectiveness of the self-help approach is shown by the growth of groups covering issues from assertiveness, playgroups and

Alcoholics Anonymous to gay activism and anti-road lobbies. There is a wonderfully energizing and confidence building effect when we share our anxieties and have people listen and understand. What all self-help has in common is action; simple, direct action. It may be a small decision but it's about getting out of the bog of powerlessness. Place one heavy foot in front of the other and, then, astonishingly we're up and running.

Direct action can be the simple step of finding others in a similar situation and talking, replacing worries and objections with good ideas and optimistic action. You know you're among kindred spirits and you take what is useful and leave what is not. The nature of sharing in a self-help group is the lack of competitiveness and judgement, and an absence of experts who tell the rest of us how to do it. It is the discovery of strength through numbers, to put it very simply.

Some self-help groups are national organizations and others are local, and are based around a core of people who have similar concerns. You can, like Ray and Carol, simply start your own stepfamily group. He (stepfather with visiting children) was impatient with theories and ideas and all his energy went into long hours getting a small business off the ground. But he was willing to be a joint host and both his and Carol's names were on the publicity poster. In practice there were more step-parents ringing as if it was a helpline than were willing to form a group but three couples joined them to meet on a regular basis.

As a single parent Carol had taken advantage of concessionary fees for adult education and spent time refreshing her mind after the nappy-changing years. Because Carol had taken courses where she had learnt about listening skills and how groups worked, she took on the role of leader believing this would give the group a positive direction. In the end she found it was a burden.

Many self-help groups, of which the best known is Alcoholics Anonymous and its offshoots, run on a format which has been pioneered and then sustained by a network to make sure each group remains true to the original ideals, nevertheless there is no reason why a satisfactory way to share responsibility should not be worked out for the inexperienced.

Local self-help groups will be built on firm foundations if initial, general agreements establishing their aims and purposes are set-up. Questions to ask are: What is the group for exactly? It helps to write down the aims especially as the group will not be everything for everyone. What is the best way to make it work easily, for example what venue, a home or community centre? a regular group leader or rotate in turn? share pressing concerns or have a topic? and who talks when?

As Ray says, 'Groups need a shape otherwise it gets negative with people moaning on about how difficult the stepchildren are and not wanting to take any responsibility for the group let alone themselves. People tended to come at crisis moments and they needed to off-load. They often said we were the last resort and they got a lot out of it because no-one judges.' Ray himself saw patterns in other couples' situations which helped him see reasons for his own feelings. 'When the step-parent moves into the parent's home they are the one – doesn't matter if it's a man or a woman – who feels a bit of a victim, not in as strong a position. That's how I saw it. And we need to feel more included.' For Carol it was too much of a conflict being part of the group and its leader. She was responding to others rather than being able to air her own dilemmas. Ray and Carol met through a single-parent network, founded to provide a social life (even on the proverbial shoestring) for single parents and their children. So perhaps there is something to learn from that even if it's that sharing hard times can be fun. There's no reason why stepfamilies within the same area cannot have a social group. As well as having a day or evening out, it can be instructive meeting others in similar situations.

The single-parent network had provided entertainment and support with meeting people of like experience. 'I had a terrific social life with lots of divorced friends. Half a dozen of us would go on a picnic, as none of us had much money, I was on benefits then. Our weekend evening would be a few bottles of wine at someone's house and the kids would play and we'd all sleep over. Mums in one room, kids in another, dads on the sitting-room floor.' Is there a place for a purely social or activity-based stepfamily network? If there is, why not set one up.

The advantages of self-help are:

- Shared concerns
- Confidence building
- From powerlessness to action
- Issue based or social network

Network Organizations

If STEPFAMILY is the most identifiable organization and support network for the stepfamily, there are several others which provide help and contacts. These are not specifically directed to stepfamilies but deal with relationships, being a parent, questioning old ways and pondering new ways of living, and how to live peacefully in families.

STEPFAMILY, the National Stepfamily Association, was founded in 1983 to support all the members of a stepfamily, adults and children, each with their different perspective of the same situation.

These are STEPFAMILY's aims:

1. to provide information and guidance to all stepfamilies
2. to encourage greater awareness of some of the difficulties for stepfamilies
3. to publicize the concerns of stepfamilies and make them known to policy makers.
4. to encourage research and information on remarriage and stepfamily life

The aims use wonderfully positive words such as promote, support, encourage. The organization is not just a talking shop but is practical, getting out there to influence government policy and to get stepfamilies noticed.

They publish a quarterly newsletter, one for the adults and one for the children which covers issues in a realistic and human way so that you can see how other families deal with stepfamily concerns. Book lists are updated regularly and the association also sets up conferences, campaigns on issues related specifically to the stepfamily and provides information.

Perhaps the first time members actively use the association is when they ring a contact person. This is a local member who is willing to listen sympathetically. There is also a national helpline which provides a counselling service. The phone number is listed at the back of this book.

Ann is a contact person for stepfamilies in the area outside her local town as well. Many of those who call her are referred by Relate (who offer counselling to couples who have difficulties in their relationships) and she also gives them information about STEPFAMILY. Ann describes herself as someone who, '*always tries to have forethought, trying to be one step ahead.*' She saw the STEPFAMILY address while reading a book on child psychology.

Her own family consists of her and her nine-year-old daughter and, although she has a man in her life (he doesn't have children), they do not live together. She prefers to take it slowly as, 'Anything I do is going to affect my daughter. I can't have more children so, I do think before I act.'

This is why Ann became involved ahead of being what others would call a stepfamily. The term, of course, is elastic and every parent who has a lover, boy friend, girl friend, partner, whatever word you use, will realize that that adult will affect the parent and child family, if sometimes only indirectly.

Ann feels she has learnt a lot from being at the end of the phone, listening to the worries which stepfamilies have experienced once they have taken the plunge to live together. 'It shows me what I'm glad I do and don't do and I find being a contact person worthwhile as it definitely makes a difference. It often sounds so complicated at first and that it is the children who are a problem. Callers find it hard to decipher whether it is normal adolescent behaviour or because of being in a stepfamily.

'I don't give advice, I only speak from my own experience. But you can hear that just talking it out helps and they feel lighter and relieved. You can hear it in their voice. People don't seem to talk to each other and I'm surprised by how little adults talk to the children and yet they are surprised they've got problems.'

There can be a great fear of releasing a torrent of emotions by talking and making it all worse. It is true there are moments to leave it alone. And it's true there are moments to leave it alone. Understandably those pent up feelings bubble like the molten lava of a volcano and the thought of letting them out can be terrifying. Who wants to hurt the one or ones you love. And so troubles, real and imaginary, don't get aired and sorted out.

Most of Ann's callers do not want to meet or want to form a support group and many of the callers are from outside of Ann's area. More women than men ring but some couples have arranged to get together. Ann's experience will be different from that of others. You may find a thriving group, one-off events or that understanding person on the end of the phone. Or you may want facts on issues overlooked in the early days of becoming a stepfamily.

STEPFAMILY *Provides:*
- Information leaflets on range of issues
- Contact with other stepfamilies
- Helpline
- Newsletters
- Reading list for adults and children
- Information on the CSA and second families

You may be reading this chapter only out of curiosity and not because it gets a bit hairy at home sometimes. It is striking how many of the stepfamilies who contributed to this book were almost over concerned with the children. Yes, stepfamilies exist because of the children. The children did not choose and they may not enjoy living with their parent's beloved and some awful extra siblings. At times those children make merry hell or are so withdrawn that you, the step-parent or parent, feel consumed with guilt. Then maybe Parent Network is the place for you.

Parent Network
Parent Network was started by a stepfamily couple, 'because being a parent is the most important job in the world' and therefore needs tools to enhance our ability to do the job skillfully.

The Parent Network Tools are:
- 'learning to really listen to our children',

- 'helping our children solve their own problems',
- 'being firm and gentle and saying "No" when discussion is inappropriate.'

Ivan Sokolov worked out his approach to being a modern parent dealing with age old agonies, such as temper tantrums, power struggles, untidiness, staying out, after he separated from his wife and had two children to look after on his own. He founded the organization with second wife and stepmother, Jacquie Pearson, to show parents that the means exist to solve problems and to improve the way in which we talk and behave towards each other. We often use these skills at work and in other parts of our lives and these skills can be used in the family too.

Confidence and Courses

Parent Network trains parents (not professionals) to run Parent Link programmes and follow-up workshops. There is a charge for the courses, described as 'at a cost which is accessible to all', and, when an enlightened local authority provides funding, the charge to parents is minimal. Parent Network will put you in touch with a local co-ordinator who will have information on course costs. After the basics there are heart lightening workshop titles such as 'sibling rivalry'. The course starts from a belief that all parents benefit from a look at their own experience as a child and how their parents did the job. With that first influence aired and thought about, parents can think about the present and what they bring to their parenting.

One Parent Link statement I have come to believe is crucial goes like this, 'It is easy to get so busy with being a parent that we forget ourselves as individuals.' Yes! After all what do you remember about your parent as a person? Wasn't it when they were doing something they really liked or felt good at? My favourite memory of my mother was when she got up and did step dancing at Christmas, when she couldn't resist doing what she loved. Her face lit up and she looked so graceful and happy, I thought she was wonderful, my wonderful Mum not my why haven't you done this or my haven't got time, ask your father, Mum. Does a horrible image enter your mind of the times a stepchild or child or worse still a beloved new partner, laughed or made some utterly cruel comment as you let go and, according to them, made a complete fool of yourself? Well, you still have a right to be yourself. Be assertive!

Assertiveness

Assertiveness is not being aggressive and not being a doormat but saying your piece clearly and confidently. The dictionary defines assertiveness as 'insisting on one's rights or recognition, to take effective action'. A course in assertion includes role play and exercises so that you remember how to be assertive and avoid getting sidetracked. Most local colleges and community centre classes have assertion classes in their curriculum and if one does not already exist ask if they will consider putting one. Some are women only classes but not all. You can go with specific situations and relationships in mind where you want to be more assertive. For example, you may want to talk about Christmas arrangements in advance and your partner brushes this aside as unnecessary. You can practice insisting, being gentle but firm! Or you may want to stand up for your child who, you believe, is being treated unfairly. This one will need diplomacy and careful handling.

Assertion training is based on certain principles and each course tutor will have completed a recognized training course. The kind of situations that are covered will vary according to the requests of those attending. There are excellent books to read after the course to reinforce what you have learnt.

Being Assertive will help you to:

- Make clear boundaries
- Avoid confrontation
- Avoid resentment

Students on these confidence building courses very often continue to meet after the course so they do not forget what a difference a more objective approach can make to confusing situations. If getting out or babysitters are not easy to arrange, perhaps you and your partner can take turns to attend and share what has been learnt.

Books and Helplines

It is easier to tap into support networks by leaving the home and stepfamily. If that is not possible then be determined to reserve a quiet place or time to get absorbed in a book such as this one or any one of the many personal growth type of books. There is no reason why advice or counselling helplines should be viewed only as a crisis option to be snatched in desperate moments. Put aside a time when you can be sure you won't be disturbed or interrupted, think through what you need to talk about and write down some thoughts on a piece of paper. Make the most of the helpline in this way.

Many of these personal skills approaches to make your relationships happier and life more manageable are based on first taking a look at how you behave. As Ray noted as a co-host of a local stepfamily group the tendency was to say how awful the children and the birth parent were. Whether child or adult, that person may not be amenable to the sort of changes you want. So the only willing one left may be you. That's an excellent place to start. Go to the library, have a browse on the ideas shelf for books or contacts for local groups or courses. If all this is just too embarrassing, then this reinforces the usefulness of creating a space for you alone – a desk or cupboard, even a locked drawer. Everyone in a family needs to feel this place is private and to be respected. It may be you could do with somewhere to say all the unmentionable things. I'll never forget my smart, capable looking neighbour, a stepfather, telling me in the local pub how he dreamt his wife flushed him down the toilet and did I know what dreams meant. Maybe if he had found a way to talk confidentially about his fears that his wife wanted to get rid of him or his worries about self worth, then the dream might have been explained.

Counselling

Counsellors are trained to listen, to aid the person to find their own solutions and to support them in putting these into practice. Individual counselling is most usual but couples and families can also receive counselling. Some health centres and doctors' surgeries have counsellors which they refer patients to. The British Association for Counselling has lists of counsellors who have trained with a reputable organization. Counsellors may specialize, for example with those recovering from addictions, or use techniques such as visualization or role play. Some will have experience of stepfamilies and understand the pressures and interactions that are so different to a first family.

Michael and Arlene decided they needed help when the tensions became undeniable a year after their marriage. The counsellor had asked each to describe how life was before and after the setting-up of the new household and both husband and wife could hear the other's experience in a supportive setting. They began to understand the different effects their new life together had on them individually. With the counsellor's guidance they began to look at changing their expectations of what a family should be to what their family felt comfortable with.

Co-counselling is a method where two people take turns counselling and being counselled. This can be for ten minutes each or half an hour. Most people find up to half an hour plenty of time. It isn't analytical but is based on letting out distressing emotion when being counselled and listening with attention and without interruption while being a counsellor.

Andrew had used co-counselling for some years before he became a stepfather and he soon found it had fresh uses to relieve the constant strain of having a very resentful stepdaughter. 'It's a confidential way I can say how I feel without worrying so I don't have all these bottled up feelings. The main ideas I've got from co-counselling is that it's OK to show emotions. And I think I've been a good model for my stepson to see men don't have to be tough or always hiding their feelings.'

Co-counselling can be very powerful, shifting the old hurts and painful memories which we carry unwittingly with us into the present and, as with assertion, the listening skills are very useful to defuse or even radically alter those familiar dead end disagreements or repeat situations in daily life. Like assertion a basic course demonstrates the principles behind this deceptively simple DIY counselling. Both assertion and co-counselling are 'doing' methods based on clear principles rather than merely talking about, or reading, theory. These techniques can work immediately and once that happens the person knows by experience that change is possible again.

After the initial 'fundamentals' course, which includes lots of practical sessions and discussion, co-counsellors are then encouraged to keep in regular contact with others in the network and take further courses or workshops. In order to preserve good practice and confidentiality co-counsellors are asked to keep the counselling relationship separate from other relationships.

If many of these examples of self-help are very practical and skill based, they also ask participants to be very revealing and to be intimate and genuine with strangers. A lot of trust is involved and, since our past experiences may have included betrayal and learning to be careful, we need to decide when this is safe.

The touchstone for many taking a new and daring step is by word of mouth. Take a risk but choose wisely. You can change your mind too. The aim of self-help and networks is for you to be a more able and intelligent adult in relationships, knowing when to say 'no' and when to say 'yes', closer to others but not at their mercy. There isn't one easy new approach which will make everything wonderful. Find the right one for you.

Women's Groups

The first group that Geraldine ever became involved with was a women's group in the mid-seventies. She was a stepmother and mother and, as she says, actively prejudiced against groups of women because it reminded her of school, which as a Catholic institution in the fifties, was single sex, nuns and girls, with limited frankness on many subjects. However, she was persuaded along to an open meeting held by a women's group to celebrate its third anniversary. 'I thought women together would be boring and goody-goody but that meeting was an amazing thing. I couldn't believe how many women were there – it was in the country, Sussex, and not that big a village. A couple of women talked about the group and what they discussed, topics, women's issues which they talked about in a personal way but it wasn't gossip and it was confidential. I suppose I would call it the personal is political and I was converted. The women who spoke were very impressive, very themselves, not preachy. I felt they had something and I could do with whatever that was.

'They suggested that we get together there and then according to a common interest. So women got up and said things like "I'm interested in women with children or women and art or getting older, or what feminism is," and there was a lot of noise as women moved chairs around the hall.

'I can't remember what our group was exactly, more like the original one; we decided ahead what we wanted to talk about, a subject, or a book that we all had to read. Our discussion was part of our thoughts on whatever it was and part our experience.'

'I went every week for a few years and I always came home refreshed and in a good mood even though it was a huge effort sometimes to get up and go out on my own because family life was tiring. But it was completely my own thing and I noticed I got more attention at home that evening as if I wasn't that old familiar person but a bit unexpected.'

Paying attention to some particular part of us, whether it is work or play, mind, body or emotions does have an effect. And the effect it has on us is transferred to those around us, however subtle: our family change their perception of us. There is just a certain something that makes others feel we are taking ourselves seriously, that we care about who we are and what we're doing.

Choosing Support

- Get list of organizations/courses from the library
- Listen to friends' enthusiasms
- Look for visible effects
- Check costs
- Set aside time for you

If the thought of talking personally about your innermost feelings horrifies you then don't choose anything where that is an intrinsic part. Attend the open evenings at your stepchild's school, there are bound to be other step-parents or do a short course with the Open University or some other adult education that will give you fresh insights into children's development, child psychology or the history and culture of the family. If you value your experience, use it and join a campaign group or lobby for something you care about.

The family isn't a fixed item, it is always changing as a part of bigger social changes, that's why you hear, 'In my day we would never do that.' Life is about moving on, taking the best with us and adapting it with new inspiration. Find your way to be an active part not a casualty.

Some stepfamily members want to talk on an intimate level, others prefer putting the personal into a wider context. Although this chapter is about you getting support there could be a bit of bonding material here. Someone else in the family may join you in your choice. Whatever you choose it doesn't have to be forever and whatever you chose to do you'll gain by it.

Checklist

- Do something on your own
- Be assertive
- Find a safe place for a confidential moan
- Decide whether you want advice or to be listened to
- Set aside time for your own special interest
- Or make time for a new one

Chapter 12
The Wider Family

The Sex Pistols are to reform for a world tour, led by
Johnny Rotten, who is now a step grandfather
>   from the *Independent* newspaper

M ANY LIGHT hearted implications are contained in this
statement of fact. It seems incongruous to think of Johnny Rotten,
member of The Sex Pistols, as a step grandfather – even if only a
step one. But this quotation shows that it is normal to describe
someone as being in step relationship.

Grandparents can be step-grands too if they have, for example,
a son who is stepfather and father. They can be grandparents with
grandchildren living in a stepfamily with their daughter and her
husband and someone can be just a step grandparent as when a
son marries a woman with two children.

As the stepfamily settles down and birthdays and other events
and celebrations bring the wider family together, if only through the
post, then aunties and great uncles and grandparents renew
contact. Grandparents may worry that after years of being close,
their son or daughter's children may now be living with two adults
neither of whom are blood relations to the grandparents and, in the
rearrangements of lives, the grandparents wonder where they fit in.

'When my mother celebrated her 70th birthday both my wives
were invited and both came along, were friendly and enjoyed
themselves. There were some outside comments, disapproving or
saying how odd, but not from my family.'

Alan and Maria laugh at the memory and he qualifies this by
adding, 'At first when we got together and Doreen and I split up,
my mother was at pains to tell the children it wasn't their fault,

she's well meaning and now she's more tactful as well.' Yet, contact with the grandparents carries weight. We all want that essential approval and support from our parents however old we are, and, out of all our partner's relatives, and ex-partner's, it is from his or her parents that we may sense divided loyalties and confused or reserved reactions. A positive interest, however far away these relatives are, adds to the stepfamily's confidence in knowing they have those good wishes.

Contact

- Reassure the grandparents about their grandchildren
- Encourage them to appreciate step-grandchildren
- Discuss the Christmas presents dilemma
- Step-grandparents may want to stay in touch with partner's ex-spouse
- Stay in touch if you are their ex-son/daughter-in-law
- Talk about how to stay in touch and how often
- Tell them what you would appreciate

Grandparents may be unsure of what is required from them at a time when sensitivities are delicate either in terms of practical advice, financial and emotional support or just providing the traditional role of grandparents.

They may want to babysit, have the children to stay and may have talents for doing certain things which parents and step-parents do not have time or skill to do.

Most want to be helpful, want to be asked for advice and welcome information about what's happening and even guidance or a few hints on tact. Others pass on their criticism through indirect comments to the children who in turn go home and repeat these. 'Granny says I shouldn't have to share my room or my computer or go to bed at the same time as . . .' Of course, Granny may not have said exactly that at all but, unless there's some good communication, however occasional, these are under-mining moments and maybe were not intended as such.

Bill's generosity and patriarchal self-image as grandfather of many children landed his extended family in trouble. Bill liked his first son-in-law, Graham. They remained friends and the grand-father took an interest in his ex-son-in-law's new family and children from that family. After Bill's death there was some hostility around the bequest of money to Graham's children who were now just friendly relations and there wasn't any money for the second son-in-law's children who were technically Bill's step grandchildren.

I'm sure without even realizing it the thought was there, 'they're not relations', or 'it's not because they're not related'. Blood ties are primitive, and as any parent who has had fraught moments over maintenance knows, money stirs up strong emotions, jealousy, competitiveness, power and the 'poor me' syndrome.

Family Criticism

If grandparents contribute in a material way during a distressing time or if there are financial problems and they offer to help, a loan or a gift of money perhaps, this can place them in an awkward position. Helen and Mark gave their son some money to tide him over when his stepfamily moved into a new home, but it made the new daughter-in-law feel a bit of an outsider.

'When Helen came to visit I felt she was looking to see how we did our housekeeping. She criticized us for spending money on a fence and said we should have got rid of the dog instead. She was sensible and we weren't. But all the children loved the dog.' Helen, in her turn, felt anxious about how this stepmother would treat her grandchildren and, since Helen and Mark were giving some money to their son, how was she going to spend it? All these feelings seemed to Helen a bit disloyal to her son, who was after all a grown-up man in his early thirties and so, she thought she had better not mention them. The result was that she appeared reserved and critical.

Special Contact

If a parent's death is the basis for a stepfamily then other family members have an added importance. 'My daughter died unex-pectedly when my granddaughter was seven. So having Jane to stay every holiday for part of it is very special for me and good for me too that I can help my son-in-law and give them a break. If Jane ever does want to talk about her mother, well, that's natural for both of us and there are things I can tell her that no-one else can.'

A wife met her ex-partner's new parents-in-law, her sons' step-grandparents because they lived in the same village as her former husband, the children and his wife (the stepmother). That was the stepfamily. Her own parents, the boys' maternal grandparents lived in America and, as the non custodial parent, she welcomed the extra extension of the local family.

'I have nothing but kind words and warm thoughts towards them. They always include my boys in a very natural way along with their own grandsons whenever there's any family get together. I met them two or three times myself, not by design but they were there when I came to collect the boys and having a face to go with Fiona's parents means I know who they're talking about. After all they only live nearby.'

Being Sensitive

When there aren't many grandparents left, the ones still living are precious but there's the feeling, on both sides, from grand-parents and their adult children about how much to be involved. Older people don't want to be a burden. Sometimes elderly grandparents may no longer be seen as a source of advice but are more often seen as a source of demands or problems. It's a vulnerable time if one of the grandparents has died. An older person is that bit more unsure of what place in the family to confidently fulfil when family networks change and grandchil-dren acquire new relatives.

Once mothers in law were the baddies that everyone loved to hate, now it's simply all mother's fault. According to the flood of popular therapy gurus, she is responsible for every psychological bruise and scratch but as psychiatrist, Anthony Clare says, '*it's all in the mind*'. The parent we carry around in our heads may well be the product of our experience but the real ones change with age and their own continuing experience just as we do. The most powerful people in the world in our youth lose their sense of certainty with the changes of life and of age.

David's mother may be quite the robust and cheerful type. She lives some distance away so it is not a question of popping round with a helpful home-baked cake or a babysitting offer. She comes to stay for a weekend every two months which, as David has four stepchildren and he and his wife have a baby together, makes a full house. He describes his mother as sensitive to how much time to spend with the family and the regular visits keep everyone clear on expectations and boundaries. David's father died two years ago and so the vastly expanded family fulfils something special for his mother. But it is easy to see the uncertainties that arise when most of the new family are not the ones she has known from birth.

Roots

Some parents go 'back home' to ex-colonies or other European countries. The wider family then is also a connection to family roots which at some stage parents want to know and show their stepfamily. Margaret's parents had returned to the Irish Republic when they retired and when she formed a new family and acquired a stepchild and a stepfather for their grandchildren they were disapproving.

'They didn't say anything but I knew it was hard for them. Ireland is so small that the rest of the family and the neighbours, everyone, knows you're separated and knows you're shacked up with someone who's divorced and they all gossip about it. Ireland is still very Catholic and although women speak out more than they used to, society is still quite hypocritical. It's changing in the cities but there are only a couple of cities anyway. The good thing is that children are loved.'

The change of heart came about when Margaret took her stepson with her children on her regular visit home. Her father and the seven-year-old stepgrandson took to each other and even though they have not been back lately the affection and acceptance has lasted, but she had to be careful and control her annoyance at what seemed to her quite old-fashioned attitudes. 'They felt sorry for him, as if he was an orphan, and treated him a bit like that at first, as if there was something slightly wrong with him. Worse, they felt as if his dad was doing me a favour, that he must be kind to take me and the girls on. And on top of that there must be something wrong with him even so to want to live with me, a separated woman.'

That is a particular cultural background and one that is changing, becoming more tolerant even while trying to hold on to religious values. A huge step has been taken with the 1995 vote to allow divorce in Ireland and so, in this area, a separation between the state and the Church.

There's no doubt that this will help to erode prejudice towards family changes including the position of children born into stepfamilies. There is a stigma about children born outside of conventional marriage, most evident in the attitudes of an older generation. They grew up in an era which often cruelly rejected anyone who broke the rules. Rules have been broken so much in general that it's easy to forget that isn't true for all of us. We are not the same in spite of television which does give us an impression that we live in the same sitcom. Whatever the other members of the family may think of the stepfamily it is almost always rewarding to encourage the wider relationships.

Like any relationship some are instinctive attractions with shared interests and others just never click. Others are friendly annual reminders at Christmas time. The larger family should not be a terrible burden of politeness or thought of in terms of who has been forgotten on the Christmas list. When criticism is damaging then, rather than have a row, decide how the stepfamily wants to deal with it and bring it out in the open.

Janette left her husband Mark who went back to live with his parents. 'The children go to stay with Mark every other weekend so they do play a big part as they give him a lot of support and see the children so often. My daughter comes home and tells me what Grandpa thinks, and Grandpa thinks annoying things like that I shouldn't work but be at home but since Mark doesn't pay any maintenance you can imagine what I feel. I must say they are relatively good with Richard, (joint child of the stepfamily). I never got on with their grandfather and it would be easier if we talked about it but we don't.'

A supportive family network takes pressure off the step-parents and parents and, like Margaret's parents, the grandparents and aunts and uncles are more likely to warm to the new stepchildren with visits or invitations to make them feel included and needed.

Since Frank and Lynda moved in together, Frank's parents have acquired a second granddaughter and a stepgrandson. So now there are three of the youngest generation.

The new members have been a great success on one side of the family, enlivening the usual visits and making a reason for more sociable contacts. 'His dad is great, 77, fit and active. He will always come round and fix things and babysits for us which makes life a lot easier, and his Mum will cook us a meal if we visit,' appreciates Lynda. On the other side though, 'My parents don't want to know, they are very disapproving. That side is really acrimonious.'

Grandparents are still parents. It is hard for them to put their own views aside and accept the adult decisions made by those who will always be their children. This is doubly hard when separation and forming a stepfamily include ex-partners with a history of alcohol or drugs. The new unit has to trust that it will be good and the rest of the family have to show some trust and support too. Not everyone can. Frank and Lynda's faith and hope have been restored after the destructive times. One stepmother had to wait a long time before her parents accepted the child of the second relationship even though this was their new grandchild, and she wanted to forget that the grandfather had written saying why the hell weren't they thinking of an abortion.

- Welcome grandparents
- Tell them what's happening
- Accept support but not criticism
- Encourage phone calls to grandchildren
- Be realistic and tolerant over gifts

Aunts and Uncles

Brothers and sisters can be supportive. In the end it is attitude rather than age that makes relatives less judgemental. Aunts and uncles have a special and more light-hearted role than other people. They can accept the new family with warmth and have fun with the children without the responsibilities. The Catholic religion may disagree with divorce and remarriage, but that did not prevent this Catholic family from accepting their only son's choice to marry a woman with a child.

'Lily was worried about my family, what they would think, if they would like her I suppose,' explained Joe, an American living in the Channel Islands. 'I was never worried what my family thought but I wanted them to meet Judith and Lily before we got married, so we went to New York to stay with them. My sister was great, she took to Lily wholeheartedly. My sister is a single parent with a daughter so Lily is treated warmly as a special English girl, which she loves.'

When Tom became depressed, a stepchild caught up in a family he did not choose, the understanding and affection of his aunt made a difference. Her presence and friendship diffused the disruption and just her being around stopped that polarization that can happen – the good parents and the bad boy.

The child in the family that does not want to co-operate in the happy family really needs someone as a link, almost as an interpreter. Another child may feel submerged by the influx of people after an intimate parent and child life. The aunts, uncles, cousins, grandparents, and your family may have only one out of all these, can provide a safety valve.

I have a photograph of my middle stepdaughter with her uncle, Tony. They are looking at each other and smiling, the closeness is emphasized by his being seated and so is at the same level as his niece. They had a friendship which was strong and developed in a way others in the family could not have developed and I saw aspects of her, unsuspected qualities' parts other than our expectations.

In every family each person tends to have an allotted role, we think we know each other and have certain assumptions 'he's always late' or 'I bet she hasn't done the washing up', and so on to other more complex attitudes that can blind us and trap us in family patterns. One visitor who is trusted and liked can alter the pattern. Tony used to come and stay and all the children liked him because he was fun and let them do things we would not have done. Nothing drastic, but we all loosened up a bit. If only we have time to think about it some of these family friendships could be encouraged across stepfamilies. They often spring up naturally but there is a place for tactfully encouraging a mutual interest. Tony lent my daughter his guitar when she was teaching herself to play, that was quite a responsibility for me though, to ensure that this valued instrument was looked after.

Family Network – Who's who in your Stepfamily
Write out your stepfamily structure or make a diagram listing who you are in touch with.
Mine goes something like this:-
His side – two grandparents in the U.S. occasional visits from grandmother, his aunt occasional visit and warm, friendly letters. his two brothers; one frequent visitor, takes all children out the other lives in U.S.
Her side – two grandparents in the Irish Republic rare visits but visits to them with youngest stepchild, two sisters also in Ireland, supportive but little direct contact. Visits by a cousin working holidays in England. Three aunts in London. Visits to, and interest from, two aunts.

Our stepfamily included two grandmothers through our children's other parents. One refused to have any contact with the grandchildren due to their father and I not being married and therefore neither I nor the children, never mind stepchildren, were acknowledged as part of her family. However, Annie, one of her 'official' grandchildren, already adult, used to come and visit with her husband and daughter.

All in all, we had an active friend in Tony, enjoying his visits and trusting him when he took our four eldest on outings. Annie was another welcome guest and their interest made us feel good about ourselves. Distant grandparents kept in touch and, when visited, took an interest in the step-grandchildren but, and this was fine with everyone, paid attention to their own grandchildren first. This did not exclude the other children. Both sets of children had their own special relationships some of which crossed over into the stepfamily.

Chapter 13
Responsibilities and Rights

T HE IDEA of stepfamily rights covers a wide range of situations and many of the following issues will not be applicable to the majority of stepfamilies, but they can be useful as food for thought. Knowing the practical aspects of becoming a stepfamily helps to establish confidence in the new emotional ties as responsibilities and roles are worked out. This includes whether the adults share parental roles informally or more explicitly in regard to the world outside the family.

This chapter is not a short handbook of information but rather raises questions and issues that may affect you, it will encourage you think about those awkward facts that are easier to ignore, or are used as a weapon when you have a row. Some of these questions will be about how to establish a practical relationship as a couple. Both adults will have a financial, work and home history as well as a love background. How do these fit in with the stepfamily?

And there are territorial issues too that affect confidence and mutual support or undermine commitment and willingness. Whose home is it? Who owns it or has the tenancy? When do you talk about these things? Many step-parents spoke of their home not feeling like their home because of the emotional history of who had lived there before. This had a huge influence on the step-parent's sense of belonging and of equality.

Many of these issues have an effect beyond the apparent facts. For example, when a stepfather moved into his partner's house owned by her, he didn't feel confident to disagree or add his point of view, 'As if I was a guest or a tenant and had to fit in with her family customs. We had to move before I felt at home'.

You, Me, Us

Ignoring how you feel gives these issues power to divide or make couples feel unequal. All this colours the adults' relationship with the children. The step-parent can be a family member for years and still feel like a second-class citizen. Talking and checking what the options and choices are in practice does clarify the emotional attitudes too. But first it does help to have facts.

When you have confidence that commitment will survive any initial struggles, start to consider what will reinforce your new partnership. Discuss home ownership and the possibility of having both names on the title deeds for which you need to go to a solicitor. If you are not married this will give you equal rights of occupation and one partner cannot sell without the other's consent. Cohabitees can opt for the type of co-owning, 'joint tenants' (nothing to do with tenancies) where sale proceeds are shared and which will give automatic full ownership on the death of the other partner. The other choice – 'tenants in common' – may suit couples who would prefer to agree different proportions in the event of a sale. Each may have put different amounts of money into the mortgage payments, or want to see work put into the maintenance and care of the property reflected in a financial stake.

If you are married the spouse will have 'implied trust', a legal term which acknowledges equal ownership, but even so without the addition of your name to the title deeds, the home can still be sold without your knowledge.

As for the mortgage, whoever's name it is in has responsibility for the debt. If it is a joint mortgage, each person is responsible for the whole of the debt. If not, you are not responsible but the downside is that you won't know if repayments are falling behind.

Finding out information is a beginning and balances the emotional with the practical. Some of these facts are simply about being honest with each other and first and foremost with yourself. There may well be things you are not ready to share and maybe it is not the right time. Why? Think about it. You don't have to rush into total union. It can be more comfortable taking it one step at a time.

It took Pam several years before she was willing to relinquish her individual security as a tenant and to move her son from the school where all his friends went. She waited until he started secondary school. Frank asked his housing association about a joint tenancy. As they were not married they had to have lived together two years before a tenancy could be extended as that automatically conferred the right to be rehoused separately if the relationship broke down.

Legally, the person whose name is on the rent book is responsible for paying the rent and that person has the right of occupation. Let the landlord know if you have got married. Are you willing to convert a single tenancy into a joint tenancy or is this a temporary home? Read your tenancy agreement and find out what sharing entails.

Other facts may simply be mysteries because you need advice from an organization such as the Citizens Advice Bureau or through a spot of research at the library. Some facts may turn out to be myths rather than mysteries: for example, the idea that a long-term relationship 'as man and wife' gives some legal rights regarding property or inheritance, it doesn't. Even more reason to take responsibility for yourself. If you want some formal agreement over assets then you need advice on drawing up a document that carries legal weight.

Sharing a Home

- Ensure both names are on the title deeds of the property
- A joint mortgage brings legal rights
- A joint tenancy gives rights of occupation
- A joint tenancy gives responsibility for paying rent
- Wills are particularly important if you are not married

149

- Check what information you have e.g. joint tenancy and right to buy
- Take your queries to a Citizens Advice Bureau (C.A.B)
- Check written agreements with a solicitor

Money

Whatever the stepfamily relationships, the day-to-day management of money is an important foundation that will provide future confidence if handled imaginatively and honestly. There are advantages and disadvantages to getting married as compared to living together. For example, unmarried partners who pool income and savings as in joint accounts and investments will find that in the event of separation or debt, this cash can be divided in half. Legally it is regarded as a 'common purse' regardless of how much each person put in.

There is talk of the single parent benefit being abolished but at the time of writing, it is still intact. This is paid even if you are living with a new partner so long as he or she is not the child's parent. Benefits for married couples are less than for two single people and benefit rules are complex and change, so get informed before you go to fill in any claim forms. Mistakes are made and money left unclaimed by those who are eligible but unaware of what is available. Get as much advice and information first from your local C.A.B. or ring the Benefits Agency Freeline.

Leila and David, both wage earning, lived together and each paid towards the mortgage but the day-to-day expenses were shared in a spontaneous way. David paid some bills and since Leila was a lot more easygoing, she ended up paying all the extras and food which eventually she found added up to a larger share. She did not like to say anything. The children were hers, the stepchildren his and this held her back from talking about what shared expenses really meant. 'In the end we opted for a joint account and I got used to spending our money.'

What is the difference between what you want and what you think should be? The idea of a joint account implies a commitment to being a couple and shared responsibility for the children but it may not always be the right solution. There is no reason why a couple should not keep a separate account each and decide what is paid for and by whom. That way it is easier for whoever feels more vulnerable financially to feel in control of their side of family finance. The main question is do you as a couple talk about money?

How often have you felt resentful or even argued over money? Do you, the adults, have an agreed amount of pocket money you are completely free to save or spend as you please? How much do you use the fear of bills and imminent poverty as a form of control? Yes, the lack of sufficient money is frightening but your approach to this determines how much this fear is passed on to the children. Do you really have to mention what you can't afford as often as you do? Expressing your anxieties can become an unhelpful habit. Do something, however small; buy something cheap and cheerful occasionally, for no pressing reason and without mentioning prices. Small acts may lead to a big improvement.

- Keep discussions between adults
- Explain family finance to children in simple and practical terms
- Decide how much to share and how much to keep separate
- Agree a fixed amount for each adult's personal spending
- Use free advice from helplines and C.A.B.s
- Avoid using money as a weapon

However much the other parent withholds and manipulates the stepfamily, using money as the medium, resist, if you possibly can, the temptation to feel good but poor with the other parent being bad but better off. It is very embittering and harms you and your stepfamily.

As the book, *Money's No Object*, by Lorna Galbraith-Ryan and Lois Graessle puts it, take responsible steps:

- Know the figures
- Face your feelings

- Decide what you want
- Implement the changes

'Luke (stepchildren's father) doesn't contribute. Somehow he thinks I'm supposed to support his children,' Martin says philosophically, and also pays maintenance to his remarried ex-wife. 'The agreement is that he pays for fuel but he never does. And as the house belongs jointly to him and my partner there are times when he just comes round without warning and walks right in. So that's the situation but we don't allow it to spoil our life together. He does see the children and he does have them every fortnight.' Martin and Annette's attitude is partially based on the knowledge that they are happy with each other. When the ex-partner is not happy, that makes giving and receiving money an insistence on the rightful pound of flesh. Instead of getting the emotions and the cash muddled up, discuss the facts then how you feel about them, but end with making decisions you can carry through.

When division of what was owned in a marriage does not lead to a happy ending then you have a choice, a very difficult choice. Either you accept what feels like an injustice gracefully and carry on living or you hang on bitterly to past wrongs. This can be extremely hard.

Two couples ran a Bed and Breakfast together in a large farmhouse they also shared as a home. They each had children and separated as a result of an affair between one of the husbands and the other wife. The newly formed couple ended up with a half between them from the sale of the home. That new couple have now married and remained together for 25 years and although all the parents remained in close touch for the children, the exhusband felt he had lost out financially. The sight of his ex-wife and his ex-friend doing well on a base of a half of the proceeds while he ended up with a quarter, inflamed the way he felt about the loss of his marriage. Fortunately, he was able to resist punishing the stepfamily he had unwillingly found himself linked with and he stuck to agreements over maintenance and access, but there were moments when the niggling resentment showed itself in late payments and reluctance to increase amounts.

This particular situation included a home and a business but it happens all the time that someone feels they have lost out financially when they have contributed in terms of work and time. And whether the home was rented or owned it is painful to leave and see your ex-spouse living in apparent security while you have to begin again with new commitments.

- Put your energy into new commitments
- Keep to financial agreements
- Negotiate not confront

The Child Support Agency has become notorious for its insensitive handling of money matters involving maintenance for children whose custodial parent is receiving state benefits. The leaflet produced by the C.S.A. 'for parents who live apart' explains 'who must apply for child maintenance'. If you, or someone in your stepfamily, receive state benefits and have an arrangement with the ex-partner which may rely on contributions in kind, could be goods or skills, rather than cash, then this will not be considered acceptable. You will be required to fit in with C.S.A. rules.

Maureen bought her children, who lived with their father and stepmother, a computer, believing this would be helpful to their education and was able to get a discount through her job. She also paid for tennis lessons and train fares from London when they visited her in Brighton. This suited the stepfamily but when Maureen's ex-husband was made redundant these gifts didn't count in the C.S.A's assessment. Maureen had to pay him in money which was subtracted from his benefit payments. Therefore Maureen no longer had any say in how her contribution was used and the stepfamily lost out on cash and goods which disturbed the good relationship.

Following many complaints there is now some individual negotiation and new guidelines. The C.S.A. accepts that there is a need to recognize the financial implications of second families with a possible allowance for a stepchild. The situation of stepfamilies in the Armed Forces is further complicated by the costs of travel as families are regularly posted to new places.

Costs which can undermine second families are being taken on board by the C.S.A. in the Departures Bill, due to be presented to Parliament and which will allow the agency to consider costs for visiting children and certain other items, for example, debts from the former marriage. There has been a long backlog and delays in processing assessments so, although maintenance is reviewed every two years, a more flexible administration system should be able to take account of altered circumstances. If there is a gap between change of circumstance and reassessment, find out about tax relief. Enquiry numbers are listed below.

And The Children

- Is it a good idea to have joint parental responsibility?
- Should this be informal or formal?
- Is adoption suitable for your stepfamily?
- What about making a will?
- Would you like your stepchildren to have your name?
- Does the child want to take the stepfamily surname?
- Is the child of an age to understand?
- Why take one or any of these serious actions?

At the present time a step-parent is just as often living with, rather than married to, the child's parent and so has no legal rights or recognition regarding the stepchild. Everyone in the family, including child, ex-partner and grandparents may be perfectly happy with an informal arrangement. If the adults want to change this then they have to get married.

Options available to formalize the stepchild's status

- A Residence Order (formerly known as custody)
- A change of surname
- Adoption

These are three separate options but which can overlap as, for example, adoption also includes a change of surname. A Residence Order gives parental responsibility but the child may continue to see the non-custodial parent regularly. And adoption may be considered if the birth parent is dead or has little or no contact with the child.

Residence Order

- Solicitor applies to local magistrates' court
- Couple must be married to get joint parental responsibility
- Names step-parent as well as birth parents
- Doesn't cut contact with birth parent
- Ends when child reaches age 16

Ali had a daughter, a stepson and a baby on the way from a second relationship when a tumour on the spinal column was diagnosed. Rose, his girlfriend was distraught, *'I felt so frightened. Apart from seeing Ali in hospital I was sick at the thought of the future on my own with three children one of whom had no legal status with me.'* Fortunate is a mild word to describe Ali's recovery but the tumour proved benign and attached to the spine by a stem that was easily severed. He walked out of hospital after the operation a transformed man. Ali had a Residence Order granted by the court which decided his daughter should live with him. This settles any dispute over which parent the child lives with or releases a child from local authority care into the care of whoever is granted the order.

Under the Children Act of 1989 a parent and step-parent can apply jointly for a Residence Order. If this is granted then both have parental responsibility. Remember marriage is a prerequisite if both adults are to have parental responsibility.

Change Of Name

- Child's agreement
- Other birth parent's agreement
- Deed poll signed in front of solicitor

Four years after his Mum married his stepdad, Matthew, 22, changed his surname. He was ten when he took the same name as the rest of his immediate family: his mother, half-sister and stepfather. Stepfather, Brian has a son of the same age who lives with his mother and visits often. Now the stepbrothers share a surname.

Matthew hasn't seen his father, who lives in Switzerland, since he was eight and in practice Brian has fulfilled the parental role for most of his childhood. Matthew Cole may have wanted to keep his name and with it that part of him which was French. But he chose not to, though there are some potential consequences in a change of name. 'We thought about adoption so he could get a Canadian passport (*Brian is Canadian and, although he has lived in England for many years, his parents live in Canada and family relations are very close*). 'In the end we decided to go for a change of name and that was what Matthew wanted because Suzanna was Cole.' *Suzanna adds,* 'At that time Matthew wanted to be Mr Normal so, instead of being Matthias Demblanc, it suited him very well to become Matthew Cole. But it was what he wanted. You don't want to take something away from a child and it was his last contact with his father.'

At the age of ten and after four years of stepfamily, the adults felt it was the right time to make that decision. The practical step was a change of name by deed poll requiring Matthew's father's signed consent which was willingly given. Now they all go through passport control together without a thought, two adults, two young men and a child all with the same name. 'I don't need to formally adopt Matthew as I've put him in my will.'

Adoption

- The adults must be legally married to each other
- The parent and step-parent must be over 18 and 21 respectively
- The parent and step-parent apply together
- The birth parent has to give consent
- The child's understanding and agreement is confirmed by a social worker

- A police check is always made
- Time scale varies but is approximately a year
- Ends existing court orders for maintenance and contact
- The child loses inheritance rights

Over recent years the number of step-adoptions has remained a steady 60 per cent of all adoptions. In the 1950s when divorce and remarriage were still unusual and not as simple as they are today, stigma was a powerful incentive to adopt. There was a strong motivation to make the new family appear as much like the nuclear model as possible; hence adoption seemed to be the answer. If the child was illegitimate, attitudes at that time led to some cruel comments. Life was easier for everyone if the new family became 'normalized' with one family surname. Even today it is astonishing that many stepchildren are not aware that they are just that, stepchildren. If that other adult they know as a parent has been on the family scene from very early on in their life, the explaining can be avoided, even forgotten. But at some stage this fact will raise its inconvenient head even if the 'father' arrived before the child's birth.

In 1972 step-parent adoptions represented over 50 per cent of all adoptions and in 1974 they reached a high point of 68 per cent, only beginning to fall a little after the Children Act of 1975. The provisions in this piece of legislation discouraged step-parent adoptions in order to preserve any possible contact between parent and child. Adopted children are free to trace and contact the parent as soon as they reach adulthood at 18; until then courts believe knowledge of the birth parent is important to the child's development. The court checks the child's wishes and gets the absent parent's agreement. A guardian *ad litem* (someone chosen by the court, not by a social worker) may be appointed to represent the child's interests while the adoption application is being considered. Courts vary in their attitude towards stepfamily adoption, as do social services, and if there are any doubts the court can grant a Residence Order instead.

Adoption is a decision that includes asking the non-custodial parent to give up all rights as well as the legal duty to contribute maintenance and can be seen as a way of excluding the other birth parent. Adopting your stepchild simplifies stepfamily relationships as the adopted stepchild will have the same rights regarding inheritance, as he or she will legally be a child of the family. Adopting is making a statement regarding commitment to a child and perhaps parity with half-siblings or step-siblings. It also makes life easier by avoiding irritating questions from bureaucrats because of different surnames, queries at passport control, the doctor's surgery or schools, and parent signatures are taken for granted.

Every year there is an average of 4,500 applications for stepfamily adoption. Joe and Judith have been together for six years and in 1991 they adopted Lily, Judith's nine-year-old daughter. Joe explains why and how. 'Lily's father left when she was about 12 months old so she had no memory of knowing him. We've always got on well although I wasn't used to children. After I had been dating Judith for a year I moved into her house and we started talking about marriage. Before we got married, I took Judith and Lily home to meet my family in New York. My sisters treated Lily as a niece, which she loved, I think she had been worried about what my family would think of her.'

'Everything was upfront with Lily, I wanted to adopt for legal and emotional reasons. Lily wanted to be adopted and become a Connor like her mother and me. The social worker had a private visit with each of us and they checked everything, criminal record, the lot. It was a great day when it happened, like a wedding, with a magistrate and a certificate. Afterwards we went out for a meal to celebrate.'

'I think it healed a feeling of abandonment by her own father. I was surprised at how pleased she was with her name change.' *And now there's another child, Emma, and they are simply sisters.*

It may feel more than a little strange after however many years of love and care to be applying to adopt your own child. This will be a joint decision and a joint action giving the two adults in the stepfamily an equal role in the child's life. Adopting is a practical decision but it will bring up many other emotional considerations. Ties will be severed as well as confirmed. These issues have to be talked through with the child. If the child is very young and has never been in touch with the other parent, issues of identity and belonging may not be significant now but may arise during adolescence.

In Bernadette's day, 30 years ago, everyone's business was open to disapproval and people's negative attitudes. She hated being called by her old surname when her mother married. 'I look back now and can still remember how I actually FELT (her emphasis) as those other kids called me names. And they still called me by my old surname, the one on my birth certificate. They never forgot my mother hadn't been married.'

There may be another way for stepfamilies to take responsibility for the children, if suggestions for a Parent Responsibility Agreement are taken up. In 1992 the Adoption Law Review was set in motion producing a White Paper which recommended this new less formal arrangement but which still requires the couple to be married. Further progress is expected in 1996. STEPFAMILY, the National Stepfamily Association, is concerned that the adoption procedure is not accompanied by counselling in order to make sure that the adults' needs, for example for a fresh start, are balanced with the child's needs for stability and freedom to know their parentage.

1926   *Adoption of Children Act step-parents have to be 21 years or older*

1949   *Local Authorities required to supervise all adoptions plus a guardian ad litem report.*

1958   *Adoption Act abolishes supervision for adoption by parent and step-parent*

1969   *Divorce Reform Act makes divorce easier and therefore remarriage*

1975   *The Children Act discourages step-parent adoption*

1989   *Children Act amended to create Residence Orders*

1992   *Review of Adoption Law*

Access

When second relationships break down, as they do – the percentage of second divorces are higher than first ones! – does that have to mean the severing of all ties? Step-parent and stepchild may want to continue to be friends. Other than when the stepchild has been adopted, this will depend on goodwill; legal battles can be as harmful as separation in cases where the parent wants to cut out the child's contact with the ex-step-parent.

If, on the death of a parent or the separation of a couple, the child goes to live with blood relations, are there rights of access? If the step-parent had no children and therefore there were no formal links between step-parent and stepchild? These questions are not often thought about, let alone legal advice sought. However, the moment when they need to be thought about is often a most distressing time. Each stepfamily situation will need individual legal advice if the advantages of keeping in touch are not upheld by the blood relations.

Wills

Much effort is placed into acquiring money and ownership during life but it is wise to make provision for the future as well. Names or legal status do not affect your right or other family members' right to leave property and money to a stepchild, but you do have to make a will. If you make a will you can leave what you like to those you love; without a will you die intestate, that is your money, property and personal possessions go to your nearest blood relative. And even if you haven't got a lot in the way of money or possessions, leaving a gift to your stepchild in your will is a memento of your bond. If you have a child from a previous relationship then you will want to make sure that all your possessions do not go to your new spouse without provision for your child.

Sally worried about her flat going to her husband if she died before her sons had grown up. She hated the thought that her partner – they didn't want to marry and the flat was owned by Sarah – would have to move out and, as the legal guardian of her nearest blood relations, her sons, the ex-husband could move in to the flat she had bought. She made a will. The steps to enforce or dispute these situations after a family death could be long and distressing. Is that a fitting legacy?

Making a Will

- Make preparatory notes on what you own, your commitments, etc.
- Take legal advice
- Libraries and C.A.B. s have lists of family law solicitors
- Ask if cost is fixed or on a time basis
- No cost if a low income entitles you to the Green Form Scheme
- Name individuals as beneficiaries
- You can appoint a guardian in the will
- Keep in a safe place e.g. bank or solicitor

Information

Children's Legal Centre
Citizens Advice Bureaux: telephone or visit
C.S.A. Enquiry line 0345 133 133
For parents who live apart and *A guide to reviews and appeals* C.S.A booklets, HMSO publications, from C.S.A., libraries and other public information points
Tax Helpline 0345 777 222
Adoption Factfiles & Adopting Stepchildren from STEPFAMILY Publications *His, Hers, Theirs; A Financial Handbook for Stepfamilies* by Tobe Aleksander from STEPFAMILY Publications
Money's No Object by Lorna Galbraith-Ryan and Lois Graessle, Mandarin
Where There's A Will, There's A Way:
Making A Will in a Stepfamily, by I. Clout, London, STEPFAMILY Publications, 1993

Chapter 14
The Future Stepfamily

Civilization begins at home

Henry James

Iɴ ᴍʏ ʀᴏᴜɢʜ notes I called this the final chapter: Of course it isn't, even as an idea, it is just looking to the immediate future and how I hope it will be. As Jan, stepmother, mother and grandmother, says, 'What makes the world go round is people being helpful to each other, not love alone.' The future is lit by bright sparks from some courageous and enterprising stepfamilies who are at this moment forging new ways of living.

I like to believe that our basic instinct is not to possess and destroy but to love and care. In so many traditional stories, including the ones with wicked stepmothers or wicked stepfathers, there is someone to turn to who has some small, but powerful gift to help the young hero and heroine find their way forward into a new life. Often these gifts appear strange or insignificant but prove their worth when the right time comes and they are remembered. Just as in real life all those small efforts for our family appear insignificant at the time but they have an effect because what we do does matter. Rather than let things happen to us we can at least choose how we want to be within the limits of our lives.

Step-parents bring experience and optimism to the new family and the essential ingredient, love, that pushes us into new ways of living, where other more sensible qualities would make us fear to explore. Second time round we can be more flexible and imaginative.

Two of the many stepfamilies who contributed their experiences to this book demonstrate how the stepfamily can work, how it can become an asset.

FLEXIBLE ASSETS

Josie and Alex, a couple in their fifties, have adult and older teenage children. Their large extended family also operates as a network and skills bank. Another couple, Martin and Annette, have eight children under the age of 16, and have worked out times together and times to spend with their own children. Neither of these families are trying to fit in with any conventional image but, pressed by circumstances and necessity, want to change the boundaries to improve their quality of life. They were willing to take risks and see what could be achieved. 'Don't be dogmatic,' advises Martin, 'the issues for me are not the same as for Annette, and it's different again for our children. So our situation has been through a few changes. We haven't forced it'.

Martin and Annette and their children started off by living in a rented house with all the children. They were on new joint territory and as there were such large household demands Annette stayed at home and Martin carried on working. If this sounds familiar this is the reality we fall back on, mainly because men are still likely to earn more than women. Raising eight children who have completely different values and with an age range of one up to 16 years old is a lot of work when they are adapting to changes beyond their control. Martin adds, 'when we're all together there's friction and quite a lot of jealousy. With so many kids no-one got much attention.' Now they live separately in what can be described as a flexible network and it is not as complicated as it sounds.

Territorial Networks
Six years after their initial attempt to live together full time, Martin's four children divide their time between mother and

father. Annette and Martin live together in Annette's old home and every other weekend they spend as a couple with their son Jed while the seven children are with their other birth parents. The second weekend Martin spends with his older children in their old home and Annette gets to spend time with her other children. Competition, demands and conflicts are suspended. The youngest has the freedom to go with dad or stay with mum.

This is the opposite of how other double stepfamilies work out their combined relationships and territory. In an earlier chapter Andy and Pat, who had a joint child from their relationship and a child each from previous relationships, lived separately for some years and then took the plunge to live together full-time. Although living all together all the time had been too much for Martin and Annette's stepfamily, the bonds had been strengthened by Jed's birth, a half-brother for all the children. But Martin did not want his children to feel excluded or that he had left to make another separate family by joining Annette in her home. The present arrangement gives everybody time with the person who is most important while making a certain amount of flexible visiting possible. This does depend on all the adults' willingness to stay within a few miles of each other.

'We do want to sell our two homes and buy somewhere together now we have built up a way of having a base and visiting. My eldest is fifteen and I want her to feel at home for as long as she wants. So it will have to be a home big enough or the right shape for everyone to feel some privacy. Even two small semi-detached houses.'

In rural areas the slightly larger, and usually less manageable place, is cheaper both to buy and rent. In the city these ideals would be harder to find room for in practice. Shirley was fortunate to finally get a council flat on the same estate as her mother and so benefit from the support most young women receive from their family.

Many housing associations will consider the expandable space stepfamilies require, although it is hard to insist on bedrooms for children who cannot be proved as 'full time'. I'm well aware that space for a stepfamily is one of the biggest obstacles, yet, we have to push for what we need. Stepfamilies in Andy and Pat's situation, in a city flat that is too small may have to wait for a transfer but there is the certainty that things change, at least we can initiate the direction of that change. Even for Annette and Martin it takes time. True, they have houses, but also have the problems associated with a recession and of joint ownership with former partners.

Kinship Networks

Josie and Alex have a large family which, spreading over a few rural miles with roots in a village and a town, has worked out one way of living. They have what could be described as new kinship practices. Good relations between many members of the extended stepfamily have been turned into practical networks providing advice and services for each other. Anthropologist, Edmund Leach, describes kinship as social behaviours rather than biological facts. There is an understanding that kin help and support each other, often confirming this with gifts.

One culture, the Andaman Islanders, who live between India and Burma, have several attractive kinship and other social practices we could learn a few things from. All children are nursed, petted by any mother and, after the age of three or four, are regarded as 'children of the village' even to the extent of being adopted as a mark of friendship and as a compliment. This is related to life in a small community but illustrates the potential for some loosening of the intensity of the parent/child relationship by cultivating relationships with other known and trusted adults. In our densely populated society we need the security of certain clearly defined ties but, perhaps, these need not be quite so tightly binding. The other attractive practice is that the unmarried men cook feasts for the village from time to time, presumably the ones with all the shared children enjoy the break. Josie and Alex's version of this kinship is to host Sunday lunch and invite the stepfamily to bring contributions for the meal.

The stepfamily need not be all our own work; the care and enjoyment can be shared with the doubly extended family, but the possibilities have to be assessed to see what can work. Josie and her former husband have cultivated a new friendship, Alex's adult son helps with the long-distance driving of his younger siblings. They have transformed what other couples would find daunting – two young children, long distances for access, maintenance assessment disagreements, a very elderly mother, plus older children and adult children with families – into constructive survival.

Whatever members of the extended stepfamily have to offer is used in a skills bank whereby the varied practical and professional experiences are available through the family network. A retired policeman, a bank manager, a solicitor's clerk, a jeweller are all there, at least on the end of a phone to answer queries or make suggestions and come up with the goods. There's lending and borrowing of goods too. 'This family is very open, you've got to trust people if you lend them a car or ask for advice on the law or money. I suppose we're a sort of co-operative.' Josie knows its value. These are the good years after the crises, frayed nerves and antagonisms. Josie's ex-husband books a week at a Centerparc every year and lets the family know so that anyone, adults and children can do the same, thereby having the kind of gathering that takes care of many issues, small and not so small. Those relatives on the outskirts of the stepfamily provide a bit of extra home-grown social life if wanted; the children are not on show for the one off formal event that usually brings families together and left to be natural, they behave quite well; Josie's little grandson and his counterpart on Alex's side meet; antagonisms are defused; potential post marriage moves to friendship can be consolidated.

Creative Relationships

This is not to promote some ideal outline but to see that using the stepfamily connections in a positive way brings results. You talk to people, you get things done, you do some things you'd never do otherwise. It's creative relationships replacing fixed positions and safety in separate bunkers and it need not be the same style as Josie and Alex's.

It is a truism that children just want their parents to be together and continue to want this for years after the separation has taken place. If they can't have exactly what they want children can, with effort from the parents, have the next best thing which is to see their parents remain in touch, survive well and continue to care for them.

My Dad is getting married to a lady called Sharon. I am not bothered about it very much because I am used to them being together. My Mum is getting married and I am bothered because I am not used to sharing her with anybody else for the last 5 years, since I was only 3 years old. I am going to try to have a happy life when they are all married.

Helen   aged 8

Two linked stepfamilies, a divorced couple, their spouses and children, four varieties of half- and step-siblings, go every year to a camp where they safely get on within a larger group of like minded people. Safe is an operative word, our memory of an extended family is often as equally restrictive in practice as a nuclear unit: lots of people to reinforce the prevailing values. But in a stepfamily the guidelines are being made and have to be re-evaluated more or less every time the other parents or family members are in touch. Therefore there is more flexibility and there can be more choice.

Gatherings

Getting together within a larger group, whether this is on holiday or at a celebration, creates a place where the step-siblings can compete all day and well into the evening and have their rough edges smoothed by seeing the adults talk to each other. For the children above the divided loyalties fade or at least gain both parents' attention for a week where all the parents are available.

These stepfamilies hadn't gone as far as Josie and Alex in cultivating family assets but the fact that they have arranged to holiday at the same camp demonstrates the other way of co-operating. Camping, up or down market, seems to be the popular option for get-togethers and, in larger families, can be affordable.

Once we've chosen that man or woman to be our partner, at some point we must raise our eyes and see the massed ranks of his, and now our family. They come as a package, even if he or she hates the memory of them they exist as part of his, perhaps hidden attitudes, to family. Many of them can be ignored but not always. As family they affect the core stepfamily through the ex-partners, their siblings, parents and the stepchildren.

Gatherings are purgative, a dose of adrenalin flushing out the uptight reservations. Ingmar Bergman made a film, *Fanny and Alexander*, about a family gathering for Christmas, the kind of traditional Victorian large family with dozens of uncles and aunts and also mistresses and second husbands and children. Not a gloomy film or a sentimental film but a rich, complex film full of vitality as no character could step aside from being affected by the others. Flashbacks gave potted histories of relationships so we could settle into enjoying every twist and turn of who was connected and why.

Meeting is making contact and contact is creating energy. Meeting is of minds as well and can be over distances, it is being willing to explore and it has a particular power when we have that shared history and emotional links. Although some become step-parents at a young age, for the majority it happens when we feel that we have acquired some maturity. As adults who have moved up the family hierarchy we know that we do have some choices and some influences on our lives. The tolerance we've gained can be applied to our wider stepfamily. If we look we will see the same old stuff but in a new light, the light of potential.

These Could Be Some Of Your Assets

- Share childcare
- Time as a couple

- Part-time large families
- Gatherings and celebrations
- Skills bank
- Share holidays
- Share family pressures

New ways of living are flexible enough for a home base and homely places to go and stay, for quiet spaces to suit parent and child or two adults, and for children who are not technically relatives to be more than friends. Kinship is a good word. It includes individuals in a group that shares common needs and loyalties. Kin are related but not necessarily through blood. There are couples in their forties and fifties, and whose sons and daughters have moved away from the family home.

'I suppose we're not really what you're looking for, are we?' offered Gary. 'Our children are grown-up, were grown-up when we met, they don't live here anymore.' Madeline carried on regardless, 'Gary is the most approved of man I've ever had. Daisy, my daughter, always tried to oust any boyfriend or she didn't like them that much. But she thinks Gary's OK and at her birthday party she announced that she and Juliet were stepsisters and they were so happy about it.' Gary and Madeline have been together for four years and their daughters are in their 20s. Daisy and Juliet have chosen to be linked to each other and not just because their parents share a home. Their studies and work are not anywhere near each other, it's just that it's never too late to have and enjoy added family or acquire kin.

New Family – New Word

Whether the word stepfamily will be kept will depend on those growing up in one. There are all kinds of ways of avoiding the old tag of stepfamily with its, still, pejorative overtone but will the Americanisms be any improvement; blended families, reconstituted or combined families. Second family is a practical description, extended family is also realistic. 'My children don't want to be called a stepfamily, we're a household, according to them,' Jenny says. Somehow stepfamily does stick; it is quicker to say and easier to add step to every member. After the liberated woman and the new man we could have the 'new family.' New family in the sense that it is the ideas behind the people that name it and can encompass step and other families. But who knows? The real question is what will 'it' be like in practice?

We are moving towards a more honest and co-operative family, away from the twin prisons of gender roles. The father out to work earning the wage and the mother at home caring for the family may have been finished off by the recession with the move towards self-employment and short-term contracts. In reality unemployed men have existed before and many women had to work. Now both men and women want a life that includes home, children and work. This has led to a huge burden because there is no limit, we think we ought to be able to do everything and the lazy, spontaneous times seem to have disappeared.

It is clear to children that adults are imperfect because they spend time with their children. Dad isn't always at work and home on the 5.30 train. He may be self-employed, or unemployed. Mum is out to work too, and work at home is shared. Adults and children are closer in the informal way they talk to each other and in the space they share – children do not necessarily go to bed early – and all members spend more time in the home.

In every aspect of life the move is towards support and networks; self-help through shared experience. Bruno Bettelheim, who coined the indispensable phrase, 'a good enough parent' explains, in the book of that same name, how an over-critical attitude and unrealistic expectations of the family (stepfamily) can destroy the support structure within. In other words it's normal for family life to have disagreements and ups and downs but we still need to encourage each other.

What we can do is recognize that rich resources, both emotional and practical, exist in our stepfamily. Out of all the families who were so willing to talk over the choices in creating a second family the ones who left a positive impression had strong ideas with plenty of energy. The feeling was that something was going on.

As Papernow's guidelines of the stepfamily cycle showed, in the later stages there was a core security secured through willingness to work with the actual situations and complicated emotions. In these families people talked to each other, weren't afraid to be themselves, cared but didn't try to be impossibly good and didn't try so hard that you could hear the strain, where disagreement was not fatal.

What the adults feel about their family is passed onto the children and colours their view. If the adults are anxious or defensive as an approach to life or good humoured and calm that flavours the stepfamily mixture. When we come to a stepfamily with experience of loss and sometimes anger these are passed on to the new situation, unwittingly, if we don't acknowledge that is how we feel. It is that old adage of 'not what you do but how you do it'. It isn't appropriate to be always full of cheerfulness either, it's appropriate at times to be quiet and reflective.

Like other minorities, we become 'normal' by accepting that it's OK to be the way we are, that being a stepfamily is not an aberration or a deviation, not a repair job. On the contrary stating our existence and being aware that there are other families like ours gives us strength and confidence to explore the options of a different kinship.

Stepfamilies are the basis of a new family responding and adapting to change. It is rarely possible to choose the ideal but it is always possible to explore what lies within our situation. Successful stepfamilies are achieved not imposed.

Useful Addresses

ADFAM National
Chapel House
London EC1N 8ND
helpline 0171 405 3923
Monday to Friday 10 a.m. – 5 p.m.
for the family and friends of drug users, offering confidential
support and information

AL-ANON Family Groups
61 Great Dover St
London SE1 4YS
24-hour confidential helpline U.K. & Eire
0171 403 0888
help and support for relatives includes ALATEEN for teenagers
affected by the drinking problem of a relative

British Association for Counselling
1 Regents Place
Rugby, Warwickshire CV21 2PJ
01788 550899
BAC provides information on the range of emotional counselling.
Can send lists of counsellors in the locality on receipt of A5 s.a.e

Benefits Agency
DSS Freeline Social Security
0800 666555 Mon – Fri 9.30–3.30
Responsible for paying social security benefits. Local phone
numbers in telephone directory

Child Support Agency
National Enquiry Line
0345 133 133 local rate charges
Mon – Fri 8.30–6
New system for child maintenance operated by government agency was introduced on 5 April 1993

Citizens Advice Bureaux (CAB)
local addresses and tel. nos. in telephone directory
Free, confidential & impartial advice & information on every subject

Exploring Parenthood (EP)
Latimer Education Centre
194 Freston Road
London W10 6TT
0181 960 1678
provides professional support & advice to all parents. Easy access to support and advice can help prevent problems from developing into crises

Families Need Fathers
134 Curtain Road
London EC2A 3AR
0171 613 5060
24-hour recorded information
regional contact numbers
0181 886 0970
a registered charity offering advice, support, representation (particularly non custodials) in maintaining a sound parent/child relationship in divorce/separation

Family Welfare Association
501–505 Kingsland Road
London E8 4AU
0171 254 6251
Assists families to overcome effects of poverty. Provides practical, emotional and financial support

Grandparents Federation

Moot House
Stow, Harlow, Essex CM20 3AG
01279 444964

helps grandparents keep in touch after divorce or separation. Provides lists of local volunteer supporters and local solicitors if rights need to be explored

Home Start UK

2 Salisbury Road
Leicester LE7 7QR
0116 2339955
Mon – Fri: office hours

Volunteers offer support, friendship and practical help to young families under stress in their own homes to prevent family crisis and breakdown

Law Centres Federation

Duchess House
18–19 Warren Street
London W1P 5DB
0171 387 8570
Mon – Fri: office hours

55 UK Law Centres provide independent free legal advice and representation to those in local area. Local addresses/tel no. in telephone directory

MATCH mothers apart from their children

c/o B.M. Problems,
London WC1N 3XX
Support groups meet locally

National Debtline

0121 359 3562

National Debtline 0121 359 8501

Mon and Thurs 10–4

Tues and Weds 2–7

Expert advice & support from the Birmingham Settlement to enable callers to tackle debts in an informed & proactive way. (England & Wales)

National Family Mediation

9 Tavistock Place,

London WC1H 9SN

0171 383 5993

Scotland 0131 220 1610

Mon – Fri: 9.30–5

non profit making with 66 affiliated services in UK. Helps separating/divorcing couples over arrangements particularly regarding children

Parentline

Westbury House

57 Hart Road

Thundersley

Essex SS7 3PP

helpline 01268 75077

Mon – Fri 9a.m. – 6 p.m.

Sat 10 a.m. – 2 p.m.

Support for parents under stress and so helps a family care for its children

Parent Network

44–46 Caversham Road

London NW5 2DS

tel 0171 485 8535

Mon – Fri: office hours

Runs Parent Link programmes which offer ways to make changes and improve family relationships

Re-Evaluation Co-Counselling

719 Second Avenue North,
Seattle
Washington 98109 U.S.A.
International centre which will put inquirers in touch with local group. Fundamentals course gives basic approaches to co-counselling.

Relate

National Marriage Guidance
Herbert Gray College
Little College Street
Rugby
Warwickshire CV21 3AP
tel 01788 573241 – office hours
Local numbers in telephone directory
Counsellors help couples either to resolve their difficulties or separate with minimum hurt.

STEPFAMILY

Chapel House
18 Hatton Place
London EC1 8RU
office 0171 209 2460
counselling service 0171 209 2464
Mon – Fri 2–5 or 7–10 p.m.
Send A4 s.a.e. for information
National charity offering practical advice and support to stepfamilies. Publicizes stepfamily concerns and encourages research.

Survivors of Sexual Abuse

Feltham Open Door project
The Debrome Building
Boundaries Road, Feltham RW13 5DT
helpline 0181 890 4732
Counselling, self help groups and 24 hour helpline answerphone

Tax Helpline

The Inland Revenue
0345 777 222
Mon – Fri 8.00–6.15 p.m.
For confidential telephone help & advice on income & capital gains tax. Calls charged at local rates.

The Children's Legal Centre

University of Essex
Wivenhoe Park
Colchester CO4 3SQ
01206 873820
Mon – Fri, 2–5 p.m.
National organisation concerned with law & policy. Free confidential advice by letter or telephone

The Samaritans

Linkline 0345 909090
The national number puts callers in touch with local Samaritan centre

Bibliography

Allende, I., *Paula*, London, HarperCollins, 1993

Aleksander, T. *His, Hers, Theirs; A Finance Handbook for Stepfamilies*, London STEPFAMILY Publications, 1995

Atkinson, C., *Step-Parenting*, Wellingborough, Thorsons, 1986

Bettelheim, B., *A Good Enough Parent*, London, Thames & Hudson, 1995

Burningham, S., *Young People Under Stress*, London, Virago, 1994

Clout, I. *Where there's a will, there's a way: Making a will in a Stepfamily*, London, STEPFAMILY Publications, 1993

Cookson, C., *Bill Bailey's Lot*, London, Bantam, 1987

Dickens, C., *David Copperfield*, London, Mandarin Paperbacks, 1991

Dickson, A., *A Woman In Your Own Right*, London, Quartet, 1982

Faber, A., and Mazlish, E., *Liberated Parents, Liberated Children*, Avon Books, Hearst Corporation, 1975

Franks, H., *Remarriage What Makes It, What Breaks It*, London, Bodley Head, 1988

Galbraith-Ryan, L., and Graessle, L., *Money's No Object*, London, Mandarin, 1991

Hughes, C., *Step-Parents, Step-Children*, London, Kylie Cathie, 1993

Jacobs, J., *More Celtic Fairy Tales*, New York, Dover, 1968

Jeffers, S., *Feel the Fear*, London, Arrow, 1991

Marshall, P.Dr., *Cinderella Revisited*, Leicester, BPS Books, 1994

Moggach, D., *The Ex Wives*, London, Mandarin, 1994

Papernow, P.L., *Becoming A Stepfamily*, San Francisco, Josey Bass, 1993

Pilcher, R., *Wild Mountain Thyme*, London, Coronet, 1990

Service, E.R., *Profiles in Ethnology*, New York, Harper & Row, 1971

Index